# CROYDON'S TRAMWAYS

*including Crystal Palace, Mitcham and Sutton*

## John B Gent and John H Meredith
### Series editor Robert J Harley

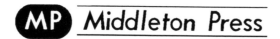
MP Middleton Press

*Cover Picture: A Feltham type car 2159 waits in South End, Croydon for car 379 to reverse over the Coombe Road crossover. Car 379 was one of four former Croydon Corporation E1 type trams to be rehabilitated by London Transport in 1936, thus marking the final development of Croydon's tramcars.*
*(John H. Meredith)*

*Cover Colours: Croydon Corporation's livery was originally munich lake (a deep chocolate) and ivory. Later this was changed to port wine red and ivory, but pearl grey finally replaced the ivory. The South Metropolitan's original livery was brunswick green and cream; this was replaced by the Underground group's standard colours of red and broken white. The cover colours reflect the earlier liveries of the two systems.*

Published November 1994
First reprint January 1996
Revised and reprinted November 1999
Third reprint August 2003

ISBN  1 873793 42 1

Design          Deborah Esher
Typesetting     Barbara Mitchell

Published by
        Middleton Press
        Easebourne Lane
        Midhurst, West Sussex
        GU29 9AZ
Tel: 01730 813169
Fax: 01730 812601
Email: enquiries@middletonpress.fsnet.co.uk

Printed & bound by Biddles Ltd, Kings Lynn

# CONTENTS

## INTRODUCTION AND ACKNOWLEDGEMENTS

This is the sixth volume of the Tramway Classics series devoted to the London network; we cover the initially isolated group of routes formed by the Croydon Corporation and South Metropolitan systems.

The present day researcher is fortunate that three tramway historians of earler times lived in the area: Frank Merton Atkins, Walter Gratwicke and O.J.Morris have left a wealth of their observations on paper and on film. In later years Geoffrey Baddeley and others have thoroughly researched the history of the two systems and in 1982 Mr.Baddeley produced a complete and definitive work "The Tramways of Croydon." The present authors are indebted to these four stalwarts and have repeatedly drawn on their work to add historical fact to the text.

The authors' thanks are also given to the photographers whose names, wherever known, are included with the captions. Many of the earlier photographs have been taken from commercial postcards of the day, and we must be thankful that the heyday of this method of communication coincided with the growth of electric tramways. The work of Croydon commercial photographer C.H.Price comes in for special praise. With the subsequent decline of local commercial postcards, amateur transport photographers came to the fore and it is to them that thanks are due for the later views.

Our thanks go to John C.Gillham for his painstaking records of track layouts, enabling the general layout map to be prepared. We must also thank Terry Russell for the tramcar drawings, and we are also grateful to Steve Roud of Croydon Public Libraries for general assistance and to David Richardson for additional information.

## GEOGRAPHICAL SETTING

Croydon is about 10 miles/16 kms. south of London. The original settlement grew up just north of an important gap with a series of deep dry valleys through the chalk of the North Downs. These hills reach their highest point, 882 ft./268 metres above sea level some 7 miles/11 kms. to the south. To the north are the Norwood Hills which reach a height of 376 ft./114 metres above sea level. To the east of the town the Addington Hills consist of undulating heath and woodland, whilst to the west, it is generally flatter and low lying around streams which form the source of the River Wandle.

The extracts from Ordnance Survey maps are generally from the 1912 edition of the 25 inches to the mile (1:2500) series.

# HISTORICAL BACKGROUND

Croydon is recorded as a Saxon settlement and may have been a Roman posting station. Its early importance was as a country residence of the Archbishops of Canterbury, who, as lords of the manor, were frequently visited here by royalty and important national figures. By the middle ages the town had become a significant trading and market centre. At the beginning of the nineteenth century Croydon was the largest town between London and the south coast. In 1803 the world's first public railway, the Surrey Iron Railway (SIR) was opened to link the town with the River Thames at Wandsworth. Effectively a horse drawn freight tramway, the line was extended as the Croydon, Merstham and Godstone Railway (CMGR) to quarries at Merstham in 1805. The Croydon canal provided another link with the Thames at Deptford between 1809 and 1836 and the company built a short tramroad to connect its Croydon basin with the railways.

The canal was bought by the London and Croydon Railway in 1836 and closed to be replaced by a conventional steam passenger railway in 1839. The CMGR closed in 1838 to be followed by the abandonment of the SIR in 1846. Other railways soon opened and the town expanded rapidly during the rest of the century to reach a population of some 134,000 by 1901.

Between 1879 and 1882 the Croydon Tramways Company, formed by local entrepreneurs, established routes from Thornton Heath to Crown Hill and Addiscombe, and from High Street to the Red Deer at South Croydon. The High Street was too narrow for this section to be linked to the other routes. Meanwhile the Norwood and District Tramways Company obtained powers to build tramways to serve South Norwood and Woodside. Subsequently the two companies were amalgamated with the new lines opening in 1883. Unfortunately the extensions reduced the system's profitability and several sections soon closed.

By the late 1890s Croydon Corporation was anxious to see the tramways improved and electrified. They purchased the undertaking and entered into an agreement with the British Thomson Houston Company to electrify the system, and with the British Electric Traction Company to operate it under lease. The electric tramways covered the remaining sections of horse tramway including a link through the recently widened High Street, and with extensions to Norbury and Purley. The lines opened in stages during 1901 and 1902.

Meanwhile the neighbouring local authorities, Penge to the east, and Croydon RDC to the west, also sought powers to introduce electric tramways. The BET company saw the potential of extension into these areas of growing population and the importance of links into Croydon. Powers were obtained in 1902 and 1903 for tramways connecting the Corporation system with Penge and Crystal Palace to the east, and with Sutton and Mitcham to the west. Strained relations then developed between the BET company and the Corporation, the latter then revoked the lease and took over operation of the tramways on 1st June 1906. In the meantime a subsidiary had been set up by the BET, and the South Metropolitan Electric Tramways and Lighting Company was formed to build and operate new tramways. These were opened in stages during 1906.

On the eastern side of the town a through running agreement reached in 1907 resulted in Corporation cars running from Croydon to Penge, and SMET cars running from Croydon to Crystal Palace. To the west, the routes from Croydon to Sutton and Mitcham/Tooting were worked solely by SMET cars as a self contained section unconnected with the Corporation system until a connecting curve was laid in 1922. Before that, cars had to be dragged across the gap when transferred between the two halves of the system. The two western routes initially ran through a lot of open country and had much of the character of interurbans. The SMET was taken over by the London and Suburban Traction Company in 1912 and that in turn became part of the Underground group in 1913.

After the First World War, protracted negotiations between the Corporation and the LCC resulted in much track relaying and new cars for the Corporation to enable a through joint service to operate between Purley and Victoria Embankment in 1926. A backlog of track repairs and the prevalence of single track led the Corporation to abandon their Addiscombe route in 1927.

In 1933 the London Passenger Transport Board was formed, absorbing the Corporation and SMET routes. Various route changes, abandonments, and conversions to trolleybus operation soon followed. The main road route and the Thornton Heath branch would have been converted to trolleybus operation by 1942 but for the Second World War and they survived until 7th April 1951 when motor buses took over. Some of the Corporation's cars operated in other parts of South London until early 1952. The trolleybuses remained for a few more years until the 654 route between Sutton and Crystal Palace closed in March 1959, and the 630 route between West Croydon and Harlesden closed in July 1960.

A further 25 years elapsed before a joint study by London Transport and British Rail in 1985 identified Croydon as a potential area for a small network of light railways. Proposals for Croydon Tramlink followed further studies and details are given with illustration 121. There is now every likelihood that trams will run again on Croydon's streets by the end of this century.

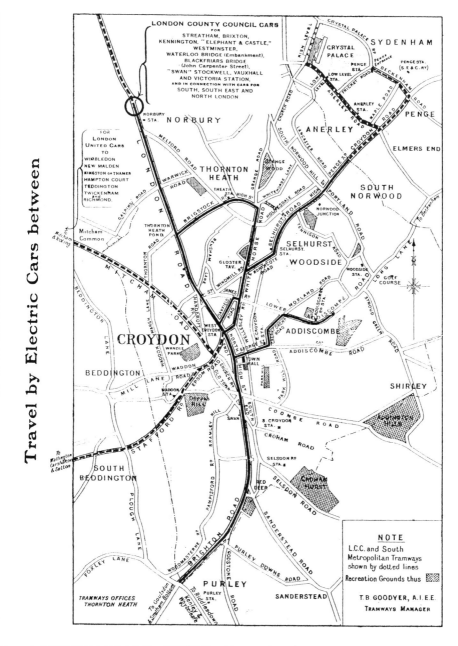

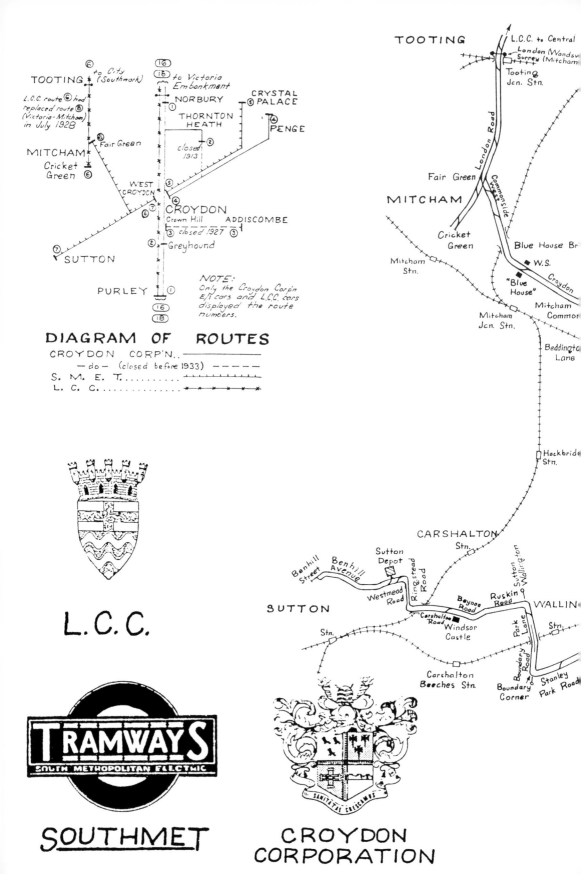

**DIAGRAM OF ROUTES**

CROYDON CORP'N. _____
— do — (closed before 1933) ─ ─ ─ ─ ─
S. M. E. T. ┅┅┅┅┅┅
L. C. C. ┼┼┼┼┼┼

TOOTING

L.C.C. route ⑥ had
replaced route ⑧
(Victoria - Mitcham)
in July 1928

⑥ to City (Southwark)

⑯
⑱ to Victoria Embankment

NORBURY

THORNTON HEATH

CRYSTAL ⑤ PALACE

④ PENGE

MITCHAM
⑥ Fair Green

MITCHAM
Cricket
Green ⑥

WEST CROYDON

⑤

closed 1913

⑦

② ⑥

CROYDON
Crown Hill     ADDISCOMBE
③  closed 1927  ③

② — Greyhound

SUTTON

PURLEY ① 

⑯
⑱

NOTE:
Only the Croydon Corp'n
E/I cars and L.C.C. cars
displayed the route
numbers.

TOOTING

L.C.C. to Central

London (Wands'
Surrey (Mitcham

Tooting
Jcn. Stn.

Fair Green

London Road

Commonside West

MITCHAM

Cricket
Green

Blue House Br

W.S.

"Blue House"

Croydon

Mitcham
Stn.

Mitcham
Jcn. Stn.

Mitcham
Common

Beddington
Lane

Hackbridge
Stn.

CARSHALTON

Stn.

Benhill Street

Benhill Avenue

Sutton
Depot

Westmead Road

Ringstead Road

Sutton - Wallington

Ruskin Road

WALLIN

SUTTON

Carshalton Road

Beynon Road

Park Lane

Stn.

Windsor Castle

Stn.

Boundary Road

Stanley Park Road

Carshalton
Beeches Stn.

Boundary
Corner

**L.C.C.**

**SOUTHMET**

**CROYDON
CORPORATION**

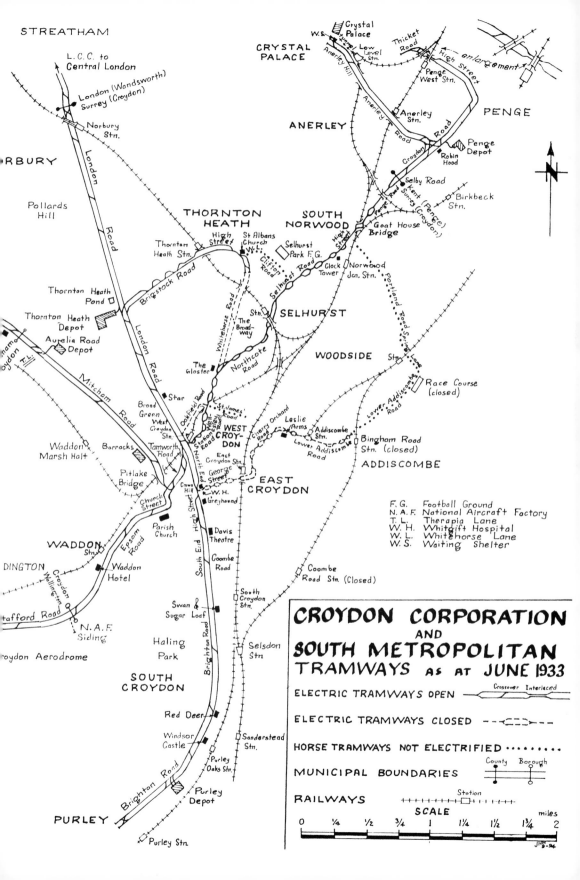

# CROYDON CORPORATION AND SOUTH METROPOLITAN TRAMWAYS AS AT JUNE 1933

ELECTRIC TRAMWAYS OPEN ———— Crossover Interlaced

ELECTRIC TRAMWAYS CLOSED - - -◁▭▻- -

HORSE TRAMWAYS NOT ELECTRIFIED ·········

MUNICIPAL BOUNDARIES    County  Borough

RAILWAYS +++++++□Station□++++++

SCALE
0  ¼  ½  ¾  1  1¼  1½  1¾  2  miles

F.G.  Football Ground
N.A.F.  National Aircraft Factory
T.L.  Therapia Lane
W.H.  Whitgift Hospital
W.L.  Whitehorse Lane
W.S.  Waiting Shelter

# 1 Croydon to Purley

1. Cars 14 and 26 stand in the High Street in about 1906. Other traffic is all horse drawn, but there is electric street lighting. (C.H.Price)

2. An inspector jumps on board car 393 as it reverses over the Greyhound crossover outside the Davis Theatre in the High Street in January 1951. In order to ease congestion, service 42 was extended to the next crossover, Coombe Road, in 1944, but car 393's crew were turning short in an endeavour to make up time following a minor accident obstructing the line at Broad Green. (John H.Meredith)

3. An early view of the southern end of the High Street shows the narrow streets so typical of Croydon at that time. It was then practice for traffic regulators to send three or four cars in succession through this lengthy single track section. (John B. Gent Coll.)

4. Car 1910 of the E3 class is about to reverse over Coombe Road crossover in March 1951. This tram's original Alpax screens (see picture 7) have been replaced by those of the less distinctive LPTB pattern, possibly after collision damage. (Pamlin Prints)

5. Car 66 bound for Thornton Heath negotiates its way through congested traffic in South End. (C.H.Price)

6. Just south of the Swan and Sugar Loaf in Brighton Road, rehabilitated car 380 (formerly part of the Croydon fleet) is working from Purley Depot in January 1951. It will join its normal service 42 working between Coombe Road and Thornton Heath. (John H.Meredith)

7.   The straight section of track in Brighton Road between the Swan and Sugar Loaf and the Red Deer had good speed potential. Car 1917 is passing Haling Park, the spacious grounds of the Whitgift School which opened there in 1931 after vacating an earlier site behind North End.   (John H.Meredith)

*top right*

8.   Experimental Feltham car 2167 was usually confined to peak hour extra workings and rarely ventured south of Thornton Heath Pond. However, it is seen here at the Red Deer in 1948 making its way to Purley. This was the only experimental Feltham to work in South London, but one of the others, car 2168, was sold to Sunderland and is now at the National Tramway Museum in Crich, Derbyshire.
(Alan B.Cross)

→

9.   In 1950 many of the Feltham type trams were sold to Leeds and their place at Telford Avenue Depot, Streatham was taken by ex-Leyton cars from the 161 to 210 series. Here in January 1951 car 209 is passing the Red Deer public house on Brighton Road.
(John H.Meredith)

10. Once south of the Windsor Castle, open downland remained on the west side of Brighton Road until the 1930s. Purley Depot, enlarged in 1903, changed little afterwards although it was closed in 1937 and thereafter was mainly used for storage of surplus and damaged trams. It was reopened at the end of 1949 for the final 15 months of tramway operation while Thornton Heath Depot was rebuilt as a bus garage. (O.J.Morris)

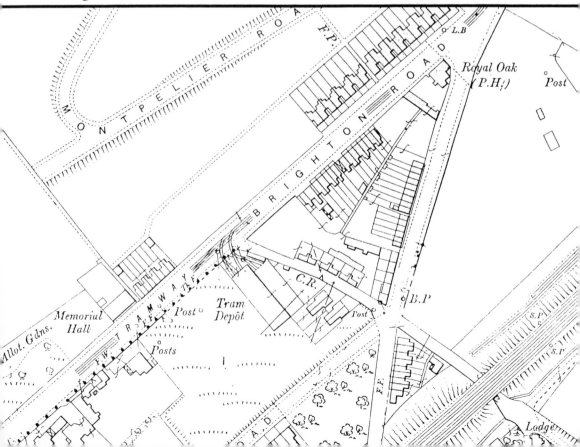

11. Norwood Depot worked a few cars on services 16/18 while bus conversion works were under way. One such tram, car 1994, had presumably developed a minor defect and is seen leaving Purley Depot after receiving attention. (John H. Meredith)

12. The date is 26th September 1901 and this is the scene on the approach to Purley when a procession of 20 trams, then sporting the distinctive Providence or Dover style lifeguards, opened the newly electrified system. On this section of route the single bracket arms which carried the overhead wires were located on the west side of the road, because the opposite pavement was not in the County Borough of Croydon. (John B. Gent Coll.)

| P.M. times are in heavy figures | Purley - Streatham - Westminster - Embankment Purley - Streatham - Blackfriars - Embankment Circular Route. | TRAM 16, 18 |
|---|---|---|

Service interval : WEEKDAYS 3–4 minutes, SUNDAY 6–10 minutes

NOTE.—First and Last cars in each direction shown separately

| | MONDAY to FRIDAY | | SATURDAY | | SUNDAY | |
|---|---|---|---|---|---|---|
| | First | Last | First | Last | First | Last |
| PURLEY *Tram Terminus* | ... .... | 5 36 5 59 11 31 11 46 ... | .... .... | 5 36 5 59 11 36 11 51 ... | .... .... 7 35 8 4 11 35 ... 11 48 | ... ... |
| South Croydon *Red Deer* | ... .... | 5 41 6 4 11 36 11 51 ... | .... .... | 5 41 6 4 11 41 11 56 12 16 | 7 9 7 17 7 40 8 9 11 40 11 51 11 53 | ... ... |
| Thornton Heath *Pond* | 4 58 5 13 | 5 59 6 22 11 54 12 9 ... | 4 58 5 13 5 59 6 22 | 11 59 12 14 12 34 | 7 25 7 33 7 57 8 26 11 6 12 7 12 9 | ... ... |
| Norbury *Station* | 5 6 5 21 | 6 7 6 30 12 1 12 16 | 5 6 5 21 6 7 6 30 | 12 7 12 22 12 42 | 7 33 7 41 8 5 8 33 12 4 12 15 12 17 | ... ... |
| Streatham *Library* | 5 13 5 28 | 6 14 6 37 12 8 12 22 | 5 13 5 28 6 14 6 37 | 12 14 12 29 12 49 | 7 41 7 49 8 13 8 41 12 11 12 22 12 24 | ... ... |
| Brixton *Station* | 5 27 5 41 | 6 28 6 51 12 21 12 36 | 5 27 5 41 6 28 6 51 | 12 29 12 44 .. .. | 7 54 8 2 8 26 8 54 12 25 12 36 | ... .. |
| Kennington Gate | 5 33 5 47 | 6 34 6 58 12 27 12 42 | 5 33 5 47 6 34 6 58 | 12 36 12 49 .. .. | 8 0 8 8 8 32 9 0 12 31 12 42 | ... .. |
| Elephant & Castle | .. 5 53 | .. 7 4 12 32 .. | .. 5 53 .. 7 4 | .. 12 55 .. .. | 8 5 .. 8 37 .. 12 36 | ... .. |
| Blackfriars | .. 6 1 | 7 12 12 41 .. | .. 6 1 .. 7 12 | .. 1 5 .. .. | 8 13 .. 8 45 .. 12 45 | ... .. |
| Westminster *Station* | 5 44 .. | 6 43 .. .. 12 50 | 5 44 .. 6 43 .. | 12 46 .. .. .. | .. 8 17 .. 9 9 .. 12 53 | ... .. |
| EMBANKMENT *Savoy St.* | 5 48 6 4 | 6 47 7 15 12 44 12 54 | 5 48 6 4 6 47 7 15 | 12 50 1 8 .. .. | 8 16 8 21 8 48 9 13 12 48 12 57 | ... .. |

| | MONDAY to FRIDAY | | SATURDAY | | SUNDAY | |
|---|---|---|---|---|---|---|
| | First | Last | First | Last | First | Last |
| EMBANKMENT *Savoy St.* | .... 4 48 | 5 41 10 27 10 32 11 41 11 52 | .... 4 48 | 5 41 10 26 10 34 12 8 12 16 | .... .... | 7 45 7 57 10 31 10 32 11 36 11 43 |
| Westminster *Station* | .. .. | 5 45 .. .. 10 36 .. 11 56 | .. .. | 5 45 .. 10 38 .. 12 20 | .. .. | 8 1 10 35 .. .. 11 47 |
| Blackfriars | .. 4 51 | .. 10 30 .. 11 44 .. | .. 4 51 | .. 10 29 .. 12 11 .. | 7 5 7 48 | .. 10 35 11 39 .. |
| Elephant & Castle | .. 5 0 | .. 10 39 .. 11 53 .. | .. 5 0 | .. 10 39 .. 12 21 .. | 7 13 7 56 | .. 10 44 11 48 .. |
| Kennington Gate | .. 5 6 | 5 54 10 44 10 46 11 58 12 6 | .. 5 6 | 5 54 10 45 10 48 12 27 12 30 | 7 18 8 1 | 8 10 10 45 10 49 11 53 11 57 |
| Brixton *Station* | .. 5 12 | 6 1 10 50 10 52 12 4 12 12 | .. 5 12 | 6 1 10 52 10 55 12 33 12 36 | 7 25 8 6 | 8 15 10 51 10 55 11 59 12 3 |
| Streatham *Library* | G4 55 5 25 | 6 15 11 5 11 7 12 19 12 27 | G4 55 5 25 | 6 15 11 7 11 10 12 47 12 50 | G7 16 G7 25 7 37 8 20 8 29 11 5 11 9 12 13 12 17 | |
| Norbury *Station* | 5 2 5 32 | 6 23 11 12 11 14 12 26 12 34 | 5 2 5 32 | 6 22 11 14 11 17 12 57 12 57 | 7 24 7 33 7 45 8 28 8 39 11 12 11 16 12 20 12 24 | |
| Thornton Heath *Pond* | 5 9 5 39 | 6 29 11 19 11 21 12 33 12 41 | 5 9 5 39 | 6 29 11 22 11 25 1 1 1 4 | 7 30 7 40 7 52 8 35 8 44 11 19 11 23 12 27 12 31 | |
| South Croydon *Red Deer* | 5 27 5 57 | 6 48 11 37 11 39 D12 52 D1 0 | 5 27 5 57 | 6 48 11 41 11 44 D1 20 D1 23 | 7 47 7 57 8 9 8 52 9 1 11 36 11 40 D12 45 D12 49 | |
| PURLEY *Tram Terminus* | 5 32 6 2 | 6 53 11 42 11 44 .... | 5 32 6 2 | 6 53 11 46 11 49 .... | 8 2 8 14 8 57 9 6 11 41 11 45 .... | |

D—To Purley Depot. G—From Telford Avenue 4 minutes earlier.

13. Car 378 waits at Purley terminus in the late 1930s. This batch of ex-Croydon cars was fitted with windscreens before the outbreak of the Second World War. The boards below the end side windows bear the message..1/- ALL DAY EVERY DAY. (D.A.Thompson)

14. Apart from some 100 Feltham cars, Telford Avenue Depot had an allocation of ex-Walthamstow trams (cars 2042 - 2061). These were high powered vehicles well able to match the performance of the Felthams. Here car 2048 stands at Purley terminus in July 1948 as the crew prepare it for the return journey to Victoria Embankment. (A.D.Packer)

15. Car 51 waits at Purley in about 1902. Although fairly new, the villas alongside were replaced by shops in 1903 as the busy shopping centre started to evolve. (C.H.Price)

16. Before bus services developed, Purley was a popular destination for Sunday outings to the pleasure spots at Riddlesdown and Farthing Downs. As the shadows lengthen, an orderly queue waits for trams on a 1907 Bank Holiday. It would be impossible to queue in such a fashion today across this busy junction of the London to Brighton and Eastbourne trunk roads. (Croydon Public Libraries)

17. Car 22 arrives at the terminus in the 1920s. With increasing road traffic the scissors crossover was reduced to a single trailing one after the formation of the LPTB in 1933. The extensive tram services and connections are listed on the notice attached to the traction standard. (C.H.Price)

# 2 To Addiscombe

18. A horse tram on the Addiscombe route stands in George Street. This section was opened in 1881/2 and red painted single deck cars were employed. Electrification came in January 1902. (Photomatic)

19. Electric car 39 waits at almost the same point on 28th March 1927, the final day of operation of this route.
(Croydon Public Libraries)

20. Another last day scene as car 65 negotiates the Dingwall Road loop in George Street. The Addiscombe route was single track throughout with 13 passing loops along its length of just over one and a half miles. The fine clock tower of Thrift's Grocery warehouse and most of the other buildings were replaced by modern office blocks in the 1960s.
(Croydon Public Libraries)

21. Car 4 is pictured outside East Croydon station. It is proceeding towards Addiscombe as another tram waits its turn to enter the single track. The station building survived until 1992 when it was replaced by a steel and glass structure. The proposals for Croydon Tramlink envisage a three track tramway station on this now widened bridge. (C.H.Price)

22. Three cars come together at the Leslie Arms where Cherry Orchard Road meets Lower Addiscombe Road. Car 19 is immediately behind sister car 45 in the foreground, whilst another member of the fleet makes its way along Cherry Orchard Road in the direction of town. (Croydon Public Libraries)

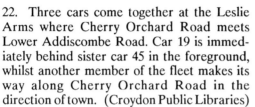

| Tk 3644 | | |
|---|---|---|
| **CROYDON CORPORATION TRAMWAYS.** | | |
| West Croydon Station | **FARE** **1d** | Selhurst Station |
| Gloster | BRANCH | Portland Road |
| Selhurst Station | | Selby Road |
| Own Hill | | Addiscombe Station |
| East Croydon Station | | Addiscombe Terminus |
| A | | B |
| Bell Punch Co., Uxbridge 11 | | |

23. Car 8 with a Peckham cantilever truck (see also picture 110) pauses outside Addiscombe Road station in 1923. (F.Merton Atkins)

24. Facing in the opposite direction, towards the Addiscombe terminus, this is a pre-First World War photograph of the route. Beyond the tram is the unmistakeable outline of the Corporation's water car. (John B.Gent Coll.)

25. The sylvan scene at Addiscombe terminus around 1906 features car 1 about to set off. The earlier horse tramway went beyond this point to South Norwood, but except for race days at Croydon Race Course near Woodside, traffic was sparse. Fireless steam trams were ordered for this route in the 1880s, but there is no record that they actually entered service. (John B.Gent Coll.)

26. By 1926 the surrounding area had been built up and car 65 commences its return journey to Crown Hill, the official title for the George Street terminus. The motorman's distinctive leather apron and "gong" (driver's licence badge) are clearly seen. The bridge carried the Woodside and South Croydon Railway which had closed in 1917. The line was later electrified and it reopened in 1935 only to close again in 1983, however, the Croydon Tramlink proposals include use of this section with a station and crossing here at street level. (Croydon Public Libraries)

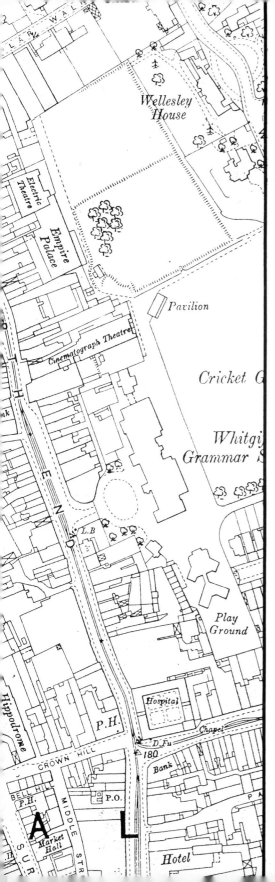

West Croydon is at the top and the route to Mitcham is on the left, to Sutton lower left, to Purley lower right and to Addiscombe on the right.

---

## S.M.E.T. Transfer Fares

|   |   | 1d. |   |   |
|---|---|-----|---|---|
| 8 | Thicket Rd. & "Pawleyne Arms" | | | 8 |
| 9 | | 2d. | | |
|   | High Level & Penge | | | 9 |

## C.C.T. Transfer Fares

| | 1d. | |
|---|---|---|
| The Gloster | - | The Greyhound |
| The Gloster | - | St. James' Rd. |
| | 2d. | |
| Selhurst Stn. | - | The Swan |
| Portland Road | - | The Greyhound |
| The Gloster | - | "Red Deer" |

## Cheap Ordinary Return Fares

on
**WEEK DAYS ONLY.**
Except Christmas Day, Good Friday, Bank Holidays, and Proclaimed National Holidays.
Either way between
**WEST CROYDON & SUTTON**
or
**WEST CROYDON & TOOTING**

| All 4d. Stages | - | 7d. Return. |
|---|---|---|
| „ 5d. „ | - | 8d. „ |
| „ 6d. „ | - | 10d. „ |

Tickets are only available for Return Journeys on day of issue, and between the Fare Stage Points travelled on forward journeys. Single Fares only for children under 14 years of age at the usual scale of charges. See "Children's Fares."

## Workpeople's Return Fares

CONDITIONS OF ISSUE OF TICKETS.

Workpeople's Return Tickets are not issued for availability beyond the fare point from which the Car, according to its time schedule, ceases to carry passengers at Workpeople's Rates.

Return Journeys may be made at any time on same day, but only be ween the fare points travelled on forward journeys as indicated by Punch Hole in Tickets.

For Stages either way between and including

| WEST CROYDON & SUTTON | Return Journey for Single Ordinary Fare |
|---|---|
| WEST CROYDON & TOOTING | Minimum 2d. |

## Children's & Scholars' Fares

In C.C.T. area :
Under 16 years of age    1d. for 1d. & 2d. Stages
In S.M.E.T. area, and for through journeys :
Under 14 years of age    1d. for 1d. & 2d. Stages
                         2d. for 3d. & 4d.    „

Children under 5 years of age (accompanied by paying passengers) unless occupying Seats, free.

# 3 West Croydon to Norwood and Penge

27.  SMET car 37 is in Oakfield Road, West Croydon. This road previously carried horse cars in both directions, but on electrification it carried Croydon bound cars only. The return leg was then by way of Station Road and Wellesley Road. In 1926 two way working was instituted over the latter section and tram services in Oakfield Road ceased. (John B.Gent Coll.)

28.  LPTB car 12E is glimpsed in Station Road, West Croydon, in 1933. The car is working on the Penge service, but London Transport were to abandon this route before the end of the year. The then new side entrance to the rebuilt railway station provided convenient interchange for passengers.  (M.J.O'Connor)

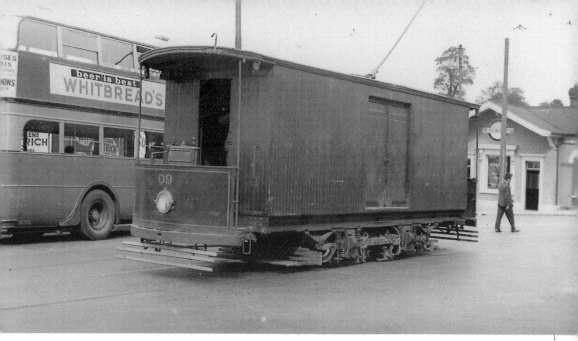

29. Works car 09 was constructed for the LCC in 1908 as one of the four class K stores cars (07 - 010). In this 1935 view it is standing outside the old down side West Croydon station building which had taken on a new lease of life as a bus waiting room for the many green country bus services which terminated here. Note the London Transport "bullseye" under the gable frontage, and the new green front entrance STL type bus. (G.N.Southerden)

30. In Wellesley Road we observe car 44S from the top deck of another tram standing on the passing loop. To this day the varying width of roadway and narrower pavement show where the 1926 widening took place to accommodate the loop. Note that the new span wire poles for replacement trolleybus overhead to be used by route 654 have already been erected. (G.N.Southerden)

## SELHURST & CROWN HILL.

| Leave Sel- hurst. | Oakf'ld Road. | Arr. at Crown Hill. | Leave Crown Hill. | Oakf'ld Road. | Arr. at Sel- hurst. |
|---|---|---|---|---|---|
| 8 42 | 8 54 | 9 0 | 8 29 | 8 33 | 8 42 |
| 9 27 | 9 39 | 9 45 | 9 4 | 9 10 | 9 22 |
| 10 14 | 10 28 | 10 35 | 9 50 | 9 56 | 10 7 |
| 10 34 | 10 46 | 10 54 | 10 10 | 10 16 | 10 28 |
| 11 7 | 11 20 | 11 26 | 10 40 | 10 46 | 10 58 |
| 11 22 | 11 33 | 11 38 | 11 1 | 11 8 | 11 20 |
| 11 44 | 11 56 | 12 3 | 11 28 | 11 33 | 11 44 |
| 12 2 | 12 15 | 12 21 | 11 40 | 11 46 | 11 58 |
| 12 26 | 12 37 | 12 42 | 11 56 | 12 4 | 12 15 |
| 12 38 | 12 50 | 12 56 | 12 7 | 12 15 | 12 27 |
| 12 49 | 1 3 | 1 11 | 12 22 | 12 28 | 12 38 |
| 1 17 | 1 29 | 1 34 | 12 44 | 12 50 | 1 3 |
| 1 30 | 1 42 | 1 48 | 12 56 | 1 3 | 1 14 |
| 1 41 | 2 53 | 2 0 | 1 12 | 1 18 | 1 30 |
| 2 0 | 2 12 | 2 18 | 1 36 | 1 42 | 1 53 |
| 2 24 | 2 38 | 2 45 | 1 53 | 2 0 | 2 13 |
| 2 38 | 3 50 | 2 56 | 2 4 | 2 12 | 2 24 |
| 2 52 | 3 6 | 3 14 | 2 22 | 2 28 | 2 38 |
| 3 18 | 3 30 | 3 35 | 2 49 | 2 56 | 3 6 |
| 3 32 | 3 43 | 3 47 | 3 0 | 3 6 | 3 16 |
| 3 42 | 4 55 | 4 3 | 3 16 | 3 22 | 3 32 |
| 3 56 | 4 7 | 4 13 | 3 36 | 3 43 | 3 55 |
| 4 12 | 4 25 | 4 31 | 3 48 | 3 55 | 4 6 |
| 4 36 | 5 48 | 4 53 | 4 6 | 4 13 | 4 24 |
| 4 49 | 5 0 | 5 6 | 4 15 | 4 25 | 4 36 |
| 4 59 | 5 10 | 5 16 | 4 32 | 4 38 | 4 49 |
| 5 16 | 5 27 | 5 33 | 4 53 | 5 0 | 5 10 |
| 5 39 | 6 52 | 5 58 | 5 10 | 5 16 | 5 27 |
| 5 57 | 6 9 | 6 17 | 5 20 | 5 27 | 5 38 |
| 6 7 | 6 18 | 6 25 | 5 36 | 5 42 | 5 53 |
| 6 24 | 6 36 | 6 43 | 6 2 | 6 9 | 6 19 |
| 6 47 | 7 59 | 7 4 | 6 19 | 6 25 | 6 37 |
| 7 0 | 7 11 | 7 17 | 6 28 | 6 36 | 6 47 |
| 7 12 | 7 24 | 7 29 | 6 45 | 6 51 | 7 0 |
| 7 26 | 7 39 | 7 45 | 7 5 | 7 11 | 7 21 |
| 7 50 | 8 0 | 8 5 | 7 19 | 7 24 | 7 38 |
| 8 2 | 8 12 | 8 17 | 7 32 | 7 39 | 7 50 |
| 8 13 | 8 25 | 8 33 | 7 47 | 7 53 | 8 2 |
| 8 36 | 8 49 | 8 54 | 8 6 | 8 12 | 8 24 |
| 8 50 | 9 2 | 9 9 | 8 18 | 8 25 | 8 36 |
| 9 0 | 9 12 | 9 18 | 8 34 | 8 40 | 8 50 |
| 9 28 | 9 40 | 9 46 | 8 56 | 9 2 | 9 13 |
| 9 40 | 9 50 | 9 56 | 9 12 | 9 18 | 9 28 |
| 9 46 | 9 56 | 10 6 | 9 23 | 9 29 | 9 40 |
| 10 8 | 10 19 | 10 26 | 9 50 | 9 56 | 10 6 |

## THORNTON HEATH AND CROWN HILL.

| Leave Thorn- ton Heath. | Broad Green. | Arrive at Crown Hill. | Leave Crown Hill. | Broad Green. | Arr. at Thorn- ton Heath. |
|---|---|---|---|---|---|
| 8 13 | 8 22 | 8 29 | 9 5 | 9 14 | 9 24 |
| 8 43 | 8 52 | 9 0 | 9 35 | 9 43 | 9 50 |
| 9 0 | 9 9 | 9 18 | 10 0 | 10 8 | 10 16 |
| 9 13 | 9 21 | 9 30 | 10 20 | 10 28 | 10 36 |
| 9 40 | 9 48 | 9 56 | 10 40 | 10 48 | 10 56 |
| 9 50 | 9 58 | 10 6 | 11 0 | 11 8 | 11 16 |
| 10 0 | 10 8 | 10 16 | 11 20 | 11 28 | 11 36 |
| 10 20 | 10 28 | 10 36 | 11 40 | 11 48 | 11 56 |
| 10 40 | 10 48 | 10 56 | 11 57 | 12 5 | 12 13 |
| 11 0 | 11 8 | 11 16 | 12 9 | 12 17 | 12 26 |
| 11 20 | 11 28 | 11 36 | 12 27 | 12 35 | 12 45 |
| 11 36 | 11 44 | 11 52 | 12 37 | 12 45 | 12 54 |
| 11 47 | 11 55 | 12 3 | 12 55 | 1 3 | 1 11 |
| 12 5 | 12 13 | 12 21 | 1 6 | 1 14 | 1 23 |
| 12 17 | 12 25 | 12 33 | 1 24 | 1 33 | 1 41 |
| 12 33 | 12 41 | 12 49 | 1 35 | 1 44 | 1 53 |
| 12 45 | 12 53 | 1 2 | 1 54 | 2 2 | 2 10 |
| 1 1 | 1 9 | 1 18 | 2 4 | 2 12 | 2 21 |
| 1 14 | 1 22 | 1 31 | 2 22 | 2 31 | 2 39 |
| 1 31 | 1 39 | 1 48 | 2 33 | 2 41 | 2 49 |
| 1 44 | 1 52 | 2 0 | 2 50 | 2 58 | 3 6 |
| 2 0 | 2 8 | 2 16 | 3 2 | 3 10 | 3 18 |
| 2 12 | 2 20 | 2 29 | 3 19 | 3 27 | 3 35 |
| 2 29 | 2 37 | 2 45 | 3 28 | 3 37 | 3 45 |
| 2 40 | 2 48 | 2 56 | 3 47 | 3 55 | 4 3 |
| 2 57 | 3 6 | 3 14 | 3 57 | 4 5 | 4 14 |
| 3 9 | 3 17 | 3 25 | 4 15 | 4 23 | 4 31 |
| 3 25 | 3 33 | 3 42 | 4 25 | 4 23 | 4 42 |
| 3 37 | 3 45 | 2 53 | 4 43 | 4 51 | 4 59 |
| 3 53 | 4 1 | 4 9 | 4 53 | 5 1 | 5 10 |
| 4 5 | 4 13 | 4 21 | 5 10 | 5 18 | 5 26 |
| 4 21 | 4 29 | 4 38 | 5 20 | 5 28 | 5 36 |
| 4 33 | 4 41 | 4 49 | 5 36 | 5 44 | 5 52 |
| 4 49 | 4 57 | 5 5 | 5 46 | 5 54 | 6 2 |
| 5 0 | 5 8 | 5 16 | 6 2 | 6 10 | 6 17 |
| 5 16 | 5 24 | 5 32 | 6 12 | 6 20 | 6 28 |
| 5 27 | 5 34 | 5 42 | 6 28 | 6 36 | 6 44 |
| 5 42 | 5 50 | 5 58 | 6 37 | 6 46 | 6 54 |
| 5 53 | 6 0 | 6 8 | 6 54 | 7 2 | 7 10 |
| 6 8 | 6 16 | 6 25 | 7 5 | 7 12 | 7 21 |
| 6 19 | 6 26 | 6 34 | 7 22 | 7 30 | 7 38 |
| 6 34 | 6 42 | 6 51 | 7 32 | 7 40 | 7 49 |
| 6 45 | 6 52 | 7 0 | 7 50 | 7 58 | 8 6 |
| 7 0 | 7 8 | 7 16 | 8 0 | 8 8 | 8 17 |
| 7 12 | 7 20 | 7 28 | 8 18 | 8 26 | 8 34 |
| 7 28 | 7 36 | 7 44 | 8 28 | 8 36 | 8 45 |
| 7 40 | 7 48 | 7 56 | 8 46 | 8 54 | 9 2 |
| 7 56 | 8 4 | 8 12 | 8 56 | 9 4 | 9 13 |
| 8 8 | 8 16 | 8 24 | 9 14 | 9 22 | 9 30 |
| 8 24 | 8 32 | 8 40 | 9 24 | 9 32 | 9 39 |
| 8 36 | 8 44 | 8 52 | 9 40 | 9 48 | 9 56 |
| 8 52 | 9 0 | 9 9 | 10 0 | 10 8 | 10 16 |
| 9 4 | 9 12 | 9 20 | 10 5 | 10 13 | 10 21 |
| 9 20 | 9 28 | 9 36 | 10 10 | 10 18 | 10 26 |
| 9 40 | 9 48 | 9 56 | 10 20 | 10 28 | 10 36 |
| 10 0 | 10 8 | 10 16 | 10 30 | 10 38 | 10 45 |

## "RED DEER" & HIGH STREET.

| Leave Red Deer. | Swan and Sugar Louf. | Arrive at High Street. | Leave High Street. | Swan and Sugar Loaf. | Arrive at Red Deer. |
|---|---|---|---|---|---|
| 8 35 | 8 41 | 8 47 | 8 50 | 8 50 | 9 2 |
| 9 5 | 9 11 | 9 17 | 9 20 | 9 20 | 9 32 |
| 9 35 | 9 41 | 9 47 | 9 50 | 9 50 | 10 2 |
| 10 5 | 10 11 | 10 17 | 10 20 | 10 20 | 10 32 |
| 10 35 | 10 41 | 10 47 | 10 50 | 10 50 | 11 2 |
| 11 3 | 11 9 | 11 16 | 11 21 | 11 28 | 11 34 |
| 11 21 | 11 28 | 11 36 | 11 41 | 11 48 | 11 54 |
| 11 41 | 11 48 | 11 56 | 12 1 | 12 8 | 12 14 |
| 12 1 | 12 8 | 12 16 | 12 21 | 12 28 | 12 34 |
| 12 21 | 12 28 | 12 36 | 12 41 | 12 48 | 12 54 |
| 12 41 | 12 48 | 12 56 | 1 1 | 1 8 | 1 14 |
| 1 1 | 1 8 | 1 16 | 1 21 | 1 28 | 1 34 |
| 1 21 | 1 28 | 1 36 | 1 41 | 1 48 | 1 54 |
| 1 41 | 1 48 | 1 56 | 2 1 | 2 8 | 2 14 |
| 2 1 | 2 8 | 2 16 | 2 21 | 2 28 | 2 34 |
| 2 21 | 2 28 | 2 36 | 2 41 | 2 48 | 2 54 |
| 2 41 | 2 48 | 2 56 | 3 1 | 3 8 | 3 14 |
| 3 1 | 3 8 | 3 16 | 3 21 | 3 28 | 3 34 |
| 3 21 | 3 38 | 3 36 | 3 41 | 3 48 | 3 54 |
| 3 41 | 3 48 | 3 50 | 4 1 | 4 8 | 4 14 |
| 4 1 | 4 8 | 4 16 | 4 21 | 4 28 | 4 34 |
| 4 21 | 4 28 | 4 36 | 4 41 | 4 48 | 4 54 |
| 4 41 | 4 48 | 4 50 | 5 1 | 5 8 | 5 14 |
| 5 1 | 5 8 | 5 16 | 5 21 | 5 28 | 5 34 |
| 5 41 | 5 48 | 5 56 | 6 1 | 6 8 | 6 14 |
| 6 1 | 6 8 | 6 10 | 6 21 | 6 28 | 6 34 |
| 6 21 | 6 28 | 6 36 | 6 41 | 6 48 | 6 54 |
| 6 41 | 6 48 | 6 56 | 7 1 | 7 8 | 7 14 |
| 7 1 | 7 8 | 7 16 | 7 21 | 7 28 | 7 34 |
| 7 21 | 7 28 | 7 36 | 7 41 | 7 48 | 7 54 |
| 8 1 | 8 8 | 8 16 | 8 21 | 8 28 | 8 34 |
| 8 41 | 8 48 | 8 50 | 9 1 | 9 8 | 9 14 |
| 9 1 | 9 8 | 9 16 | 9 21 | 9 28 | 9 34 |
| 9 21 | 9 28 | 9 36 | 9 41 | 9 48 | 9 54 |
| 9 41 | 9 48 | 9 56 | 10 1 | 10 8 | 10 14 |

### FARES BETWEEN

| | | |
|---|---|---|
| Crown Hill and Oakfield | ... ... ... ... | 1d. |
| " " Thornton Heath | ... ... ... | 2d. |
| " " Spurgeon's Chapel | ... | 1d. |
| " " Selhurst | ... ... ... | 2d. |
| West Croydon Station and Half Moon | ... | 1d. |
| Oakfield Road and Glo'ster Tavern | ... ... | 1d. |
| Glo'ster Tavern and Selhurst | ... ... ... | 1d. |
| Half Moon and Thornton Heath | ... ... | 1d. |
| High Street and Red Deer | ... ... ... | 2d. |
| " " Swan and Sugar Loaf | ... | 1d. |
| Swan and Sugar Loaf and Red Deer | ... ... | 1d. |
| Crown Hill and East Croydon | ... ... ... | ½d. |

Books, 24 Tickets, 3s. 6d.; 12 Tickets, 1s. 10d.

*No alterations during the current Month.*

Horse timetable from about 1881.

31. SMET car 44 is on the Croydon to Crystal Palace service in Whitehorse Road during the First World War.   (O.J.Morris)

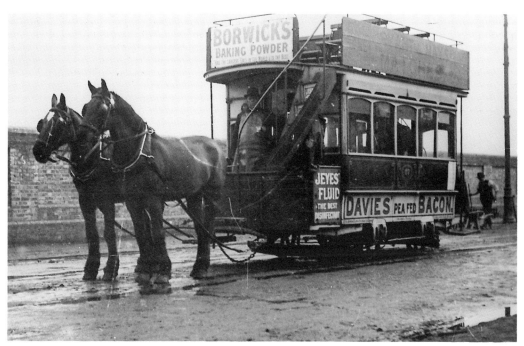

32. Electric tramway operation between West Croydon and Selhurst was inaugurated in January 1902, but it was not until March that the cars reached South Norwood. This horse car standing at Selhurst is operating a shuttle service to South Norwood during the intervening two months.
(Croydon Public Libraries)

33. Corporation car 21 ascends the hill in Selhurst Road en route from Croydon to Penge before 1914. (Card House)

34. A Corporation tram passes the clock tower in South Norwood High Street during the early 1920s. (John B.Gent Coll.)

35. At the opposite end of the High Street, SMET car 49 tackles the short rise to Goat House Bridge. (C.H.Price)

36. Half a mile further from the previous scene, SMET car 40 is in Croydon Road and is about to cross the county boundary between Kent and Surrey which also divided Penge UDC from the Borough of Croydon. The photographer recorded the time as 4pm on 27th June 1917. (O.J.Morris)

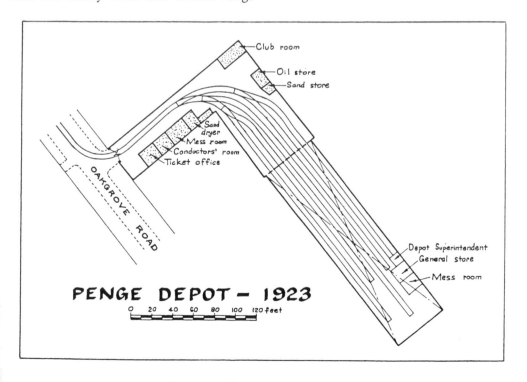

Club room
Oil store
Sand store
Sand dryer
Mess room
Conductors' room
Ticket office

OAKGROVE ROAD

Depot Superintendent
General store
Mess room

PENGE DEPOT – 1923

0  20  40  60  80  100  120 feet

37. Having passed the junction with the Crystal Palace route at the Robin Hood and turned left at Penge, Croydon Corporation car 23 is climbing Penge High Street towards the terminus in Thicket Road.
(John B. Gent Coll.)

38. Shortly after the opening of the Penge route SMET car 7 has left the terminus and turned into the High Street. The car's destination is Selby Road, the Penge/Croydon boundary, as due to a dispute between the SMET company and Croydon Corporation, cars were unable to work through to Croydon between June 1906 and June 1907. The arch bridge carries the Crystal Palace Low Level branch railway and the girder bridge in the background is used by the London Bridge to Brighton main line. The tram tracks were interlaced under the latter bridge due to its restricted width. (John B. Gent Coll.)

### CROYDON—Through Running.

The Penge and Palace lines are run in co-operation with the Croydon Corporation under a through running agreement, so that the Company's cars and servants technically whilst in the Croydon area are in the service of the Corporation, and are subject to their Bye-laws and Regulations.

Special through running local tickets are issued, and each passenger must be asked his exact destination and only given a ticket thereto.

Passengers must at Croydon Terminus leave the car at the Motorman's end, and the cars may not be stopped for any passenger purpose in the London Road.

The cars must be properly spaced using only the passing places allotted and no two cars may follow each other through the same passing place except under exceptional circumstances when they must be reported.

Altercations and comments between the two Staffs must be particularly avoided.

Palace cars show a white light and Penge a green light.

| PENGE ROUTE | | |
|---|---|---|
| **FIRST CARS** | WEEKDAYS A.M. | SUNDAYS A.M. |
| Selby Rd. to Croydon | 6.20 | 8.49 |
| Croydon to Penge - | 7. 4 | 9. 0 |
| Penge to Croydon - | 7.29 | 9.24 |
| Penge to "Robin Hood" | 7.29 | 9.24 |
| **LAST CARS** | P.M. | P.M. |
| Croydon to Penge - | 11.10 | 10.56 |
| Penge to Croydon - | 11.34 | 11.23 |
| Croydon to Selby Rd. | 11.20 | 11. 8 |

39. A Board of Trade inspection of the Penge and Crystal Palace lines was undertaken on 10th April 1906 and SMET car 13 is standing at Penge terminus with the inspecting officer, Colonel Von Donop, on the platform. The system was being operated under the Croydon Corporation lease, hence the sign CROYDON CORPORATION TRAMWAYS secured to the waist panel of the tram. The lease was terminated on 1st June 1906.
(Penge Public Library)

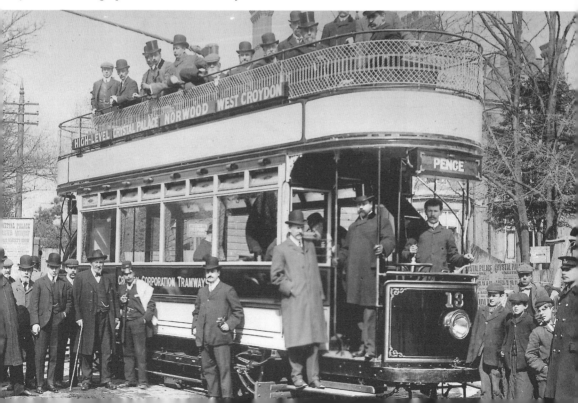

# 4 To Crystal Palace

40. SMET car 45 is on the Crystal Palace route in about 1930. Having descended Anerley Hill, the car has arrived at the Robin Hood triangular junction (the Robin Hood hostelry is on the right, behind the tram). Car 45 will shortly turn right over the junction for Croydon. The depot for the Crystal Palace cars was in Oakgrove Road, a short distance around the left hand corner. (C.F.Klapper)

WEST CROYDON

8

41. Looking up Anerley Road, another SMET short wheelbase car is approaching Anerley station which is described fully in the Middleton Press album *London Bridge to East Croydon*. (C.H.Price)

42. SMET long wheelbase car 8 is at the bottom of Anerley Hill on a Crystal Palace Low Level working. This was between the opening of the first section of the route on 12th April 1906 and the extension to Crystal Palace High Level on 28th May 1906. (John B.Gent Coll.)

43. Two SMET type M cars pass at the foot of Anerley Hill. The Crystal Palace had been rebuilt on Sydenham Hill in 1854 following its 1851 debut in Hyde Park, and the structure stood until 1936 when it was destroyed by fire. The two towers survived the fire, but during the Second World War the south tower seen here was dismantled whilst its opposite number was spectacularly felled by explosives.
(John B.Gent Coll.)

44. SMET car 6 climbs the 1 in 9 gradient of Anerley Hill between the Low Level and High Level stations. This was the steepest part of the London area tramways. There were two compulsory stops for descending cars on this hill, but none for ascending cars.
(John B.Gent Coll.)

45. The Crystal Palace and its grounds were the scene of many events and exhibitions, attracting large crowds, many of whom came by tram. In 1911 the Festival of Empire exhibition included an "All Red Route Railway" which connected various colonial and dominion pavilions on a continuous route. It was a 3ft. 6ins./1067 mm gauge line with two outside electric conductor rails. Eighteen covered four wheel toastrack cars, which consisted of nine powered cars and nine trailers, provided the service. One of the powered cars was later fitted with a trolley pole and it ended its days on the Dublin and Lucan Electric Railway in Ireland. (Rotary Photo)

## CRYSTAL PALACE ROUTE

| FIRST CARS | | WEEKDAYS A.M. | SUNDAYS A.M. |
|---|---|---|---|
| Croydon to Palace | - | 7. 0 | 9. 6 |
| Palace to Croydon | - | 6.58 | 9. 1 |
| "Robin Hood" to Palace | | 6.48 | 8.51 |
| "Robin Hood" to Croydon | | 6.39 | 8.46 |
| **LAST CARS** | | P.M. | P.M. |
| Croydon to Palace | - | 11.13 | 10.51 |
| Palace to Croydon | - | *11.26 | *11.12 |
| Palace to "Robin Hood" | | 11.42 | 11.24 |
| "Robin Hood" to Palace | | 11.32 | 11.10 |
| "Robin Hood" to Croydon | | 11.40 | 11.28 |

* Change at "Robin Hood."

### B.O.T. AND COMPULSORY STOPS.

All poles painted red.

Conductors must always stay on the rear platform on cars going up or down Anerley Hill, and cars must not be stopped for passengers ascending same. Fares must be taken either on the platform or before the car starts.

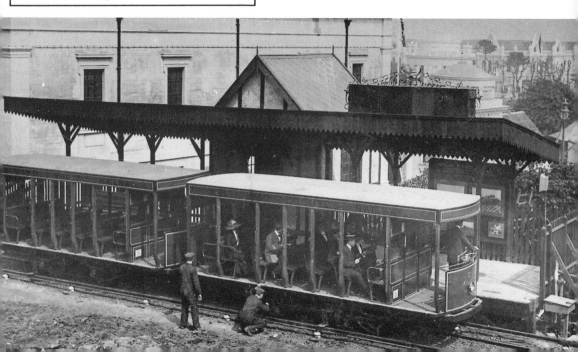

46. Ex-Croydon car 346 is seen in its twilight years at Crystal Palace terminus in August 1935. Cars 345 - 347 were fitted with track brakes after closure of the Penge route in 1933; they then joined the ex-SMET type M cars to work an augmented Croydon to Crystal Palace service. The passenger shelter was one of just two in the Croydon area, the other was at Blue House on Mitcham Common. (O.J.Morris)

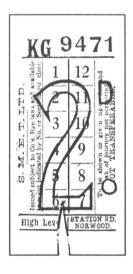

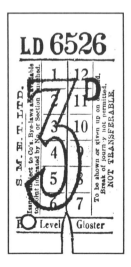

# 5 West Croydon to Sutton

47. SMET car 30 waits on the terminal spur for the Sutton and Tooting routes in Tamworth Road, West Croydon. The tram seen here around 1920, is one of the four ex-Gravesend bogie cars and it is depicted in original state with reversed stairs (see also picture 117). Note the prominent sign announcing a 6d return fare to Sutton or Tooting!
(O.J.Morris)

48. Facing in the opposite direction, SMET car 8 is seen working on the Sutton service in 1923. Croydon's principal shopping street, North End, is behind the tram and it is served by the Norbury to Purley route.
(F.Merton Atkins)

49. A derailment took place in 1917 in Tamworth Road and the tram involved, SMET car 31, was one of the five Brush bogie cars which were rather prone to such mishaps. The screen around the stairs was to protect the modesty of women conductors who were employed during the First World War.
(John H.Meredith Coll.)

50. We now observe a mid-1930s scene with former LCC E class car 450 on the extended service 30 between Croydon and "Near Willesden Junction." This was London's longest tram service; 81 minutes was allowed for the fourteen mile journey. Tamworth Road was laid out on the alignment of the Croydon canal company's tramroad which linked the canal basin at West Croydon with Surrey Iron and Croydon, Merstham and Godstone railways at Pitlake. Trams will run again at this location as part of the one way loop around the town centre under the proposals for Tramlink.
(John H.Meredith Coll.)

51. The Mitcham/Tooting route diverged from the Sutton route over a single track curve in Lower Church Street. Cars from Mitcham into Croydon worked over the crossover in the foreground to gain the correct track, the operation being controlled by light signals. SMET car 9 (left) is bound for Sutton and a London United Tramways type U tram, on loan to the SMET, is working to Mitcham. Note the conductor checking that the trolley is behaving correctly on the sharp curve. The tower of Croydon's parish church appears above the roof of the LUT car.
(A.D.Packer Coll.)

54. The prominent building in Stafford Road which the tram has just passed on its way to Croydon is now the Waddon Hotel. The area is now fully built up, however, in 1906 from this point to Wallington there were nearly two miles of farmland with no more than two or three houses. Fields of corn, lavender, peppermint and other herbs were on either side of the tracks; it was a very popular ride. During the First World War much of the arable land to the south gave way to airfields which later became Croydon Aerodrome, the airport for London. The associated National Aircraft Factory opened in 1918 was served by a railway siding, crossing the tramway on the level; a short tramway siding was also constructed to allow workmen's cars to stand clear of the main route.   (John B.Gent Coll.) ➤

52. The SMET operated a parcels service on the two western routes between 1908 and 1911. In this posed photograph car 13 is in Church Street, Croydon, and is carrying two large wicker baskets inscribed TPE (Tramways Parcels Express). (John B.Gent Coll.)

53. We now catch sight of a tram in Epsom Road, Croydon; the photo was taken around 1910. On the traction standard is fixed the fare stage number which was part of a scheme adopted by the BET in 1909, known as the "Fair Fare" system. (Croydon Public Libraries)

55. The first section of the Sutton route to be inspected by the Board of Trade was between Waddon and Carshalton. SMET car 25, having been brought in specially by road, is seen on the inspection in Stafford Road, Wallington on 11th August 1906. The whole of the SMET system was opened in stages during 1906. (John B.Gent Coll.)

56. One of the SMET long wheelbase cars is turning from Stanley Park Road, Wallington into Boundary Road. The SMET adopted similar shield type stop signs to Croydon Corporation and one can be seen on the overhead standard to the left of the tram. There was still much open country between Wallington and Sutton when the trams started, but house building soon followed on a large scale and by the mid-1920s most of the route was lined with houses and shops. (C.H.Price)

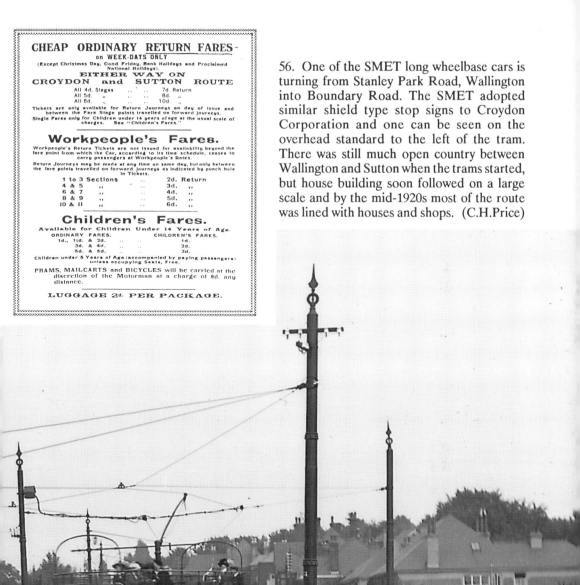

57. The Sutton route not only ran through open country, but it was clear of established streets in the Carshalton area as this photograph of track laying in the new Ruskin Road illustrates. Due to a time limit in the authorising Act of Parliament, work had to be completed quickly and in several cases new roads were constructed along with the tramway. Unlike Croydon Corporation with its largely single track and passing loop sections, the majority of the SMET system was constructed with double track with only isolated stretches of interlaced or single track. (Sutton Public Libraries)

South Metropolitan Electric Tramways LTD.

# NOTICE

## RECENT POLICE COURT CONVICTIONS

TOWN HALL, CROYDON.

For attempting to avoid payment of fare a passenger was convicted and fined.

AT CROYDON COUNTY BENCH.

For assaulting a Conductor two men were convicted and fined or an alternative of seven days imprisonment each.

ELECTRIC RAILWAY HOUSE
BROADWAY, WESTMINSTER, S.W.1

TRAMWAYS

58. At the Windsor Castle the route reverted to established streets. Here Croydon bound SMET car 38 is about to turn from Carshalton Road into Beynon Road. This tram was normally used on the Crystal Palace service, but it is helping out on the Sutton route in this 1918 photograph.   (O.J.Morris)

59. Continuing towards Sutton the route ran along Carshalton Road, then over interlaced track in Ringstead Road, finally cars turned westwards along Westmead Road and Benhill Avenue. About 1908, car 9 is pictured in Benhill Avenue nearing the Sutton terminus on the final leg of its journey from Croydon. (John B.Gent Coll.)

60. The Sutton route had a large depot in Westmead Road, half a mile short of the terminus. The sixty car capacity catered for future track extensions which did not materialise. The depot was also used for overhauling the SMET fleet. When overhauls were transferred to the Hendon depot of the Metropolitan Electric Tramways, part of the Sutton depot was used for office accommodation. (John B.Gent Coll.)

## SUTTON ROUTE

| FIRST CARS | WEEKDAYS A.M. | SUNDAYS A.M. |
|---|---|---|
| Croydon to Sutton | 6.10 | 9. 0 |
| Sutton to Croydon | 5.38 | 8.25 |
| Westmead Road to Sutton | 5.33 | 8.20 |

| LAST CARS | P.M. | P.M. |
|---|---|---|
| Croydon to Sutton | 11.15 | 11. 0 |
| Croydon to Sutton Dt. | 11.47 | 11.36 |
| Sutton to Croydon | 10.40 | 10.27 |
| Sutton to Woodcote Road | 10.40 | 10.27 |
| Sutton to Westmead Road | 11.47 | 11.32 |

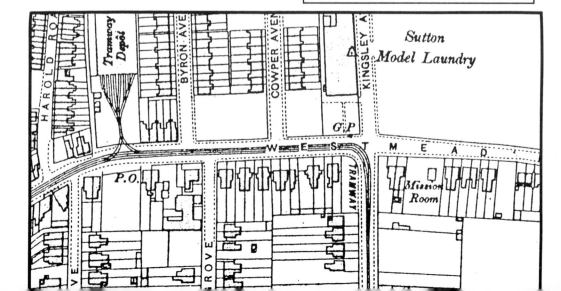

61. A busy scene at Sutton terminus on Derby Day 1907. Epsom racecourse was four miles to the south and this was an important transfer point for racegoers, many of whom apparently made the rest of the journey by cab. (John B. Gent Coll.)

62. The axe is about to fall on the trams and we witness one of the final days of the Sutton route. A former LUT type U car stands at the terminus; ten of these trams were loaned to the SMET and they were the only vehicles with covered tops to be operated by the SMET company. A number were transferred from the Mitcham route in 1933 when ex-LCC cars were introduced on the West Croydon/Willesden service. The two trolleybuses, bought over from Fulwell depot in West London, are on training runs prior to the introduction of route 654 to West Croydon in December 1935. The new trolleybus route was extended to Crystal Palace in February 1936. (Sutton Public Libraries)

# 6 West Croydon to Mitcham and Tooting

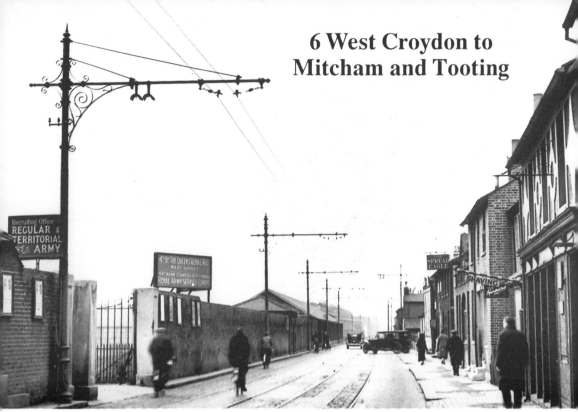

63. The Mitcham route was the least photographed of the Croydon system. After crossing the West Croydon to Sutton railway by means of Pitlake Bridge, the trams passed Mitcham Road Barracks where the tracks were laid close to the edge of the highway and there was no pavement. A short distance beyond the barracks there was farmland on the west side of the road and only patchy development on the right all the way to Mitcham Common until after the First World War. (Croydon Public Libraries)

64. The SMET had a depot in Aurelia Road and this was approached by the connection in the foreground of this 1917 view. The ornate wall is that of Croydon Cemetery and the factory beyond was a peppermint and lavender distillery. (O.J.Morris)

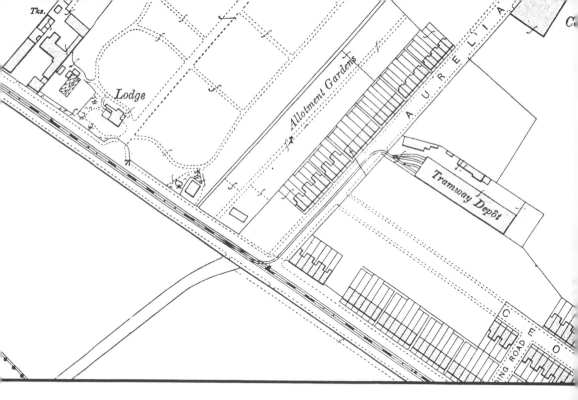

65. Shortly beyond the cemetery, the tramway reached the two mile expanse of Mitcham Common with the Jolly Gardeners public house on the edge. This was always known as the "Red House", and towards the Mitcham side of the common, the Ravensbury Arms, or "Blue House" was reached. Here SMET car 40, a stranger to the Mitcham route, has just passed the "Blue House" and is about to climb over the LB&SCR Streatham to Sutton railway line. The SMET advertised "Fresh Air Rides Across Breezy Mitcham Common." (John B. Gent Coll.)

66. In 1936, only one year before the route was converted to trolleybus operation, the "Blue House" bridge was reconstructed and widened. A temporary single track was laid on sleepers over the widened portion and carried trams only while the original part of the bridge was rebuilt. The other rails seen in this picture belong to the contractor's narrow gauge railway. (O.J.Morris)

67. At Fair Green, Mitcham, the route from Croydon converged with the projected Mitcham to Sutton line which got no further than a half a mile section to the Cricket Green. This was operated by a SMET shuttle car for a few years; it then fell into disuse until revived later for operation by LCC cars. Here SMET car 23, one of the Milnes built trams, is bound from Croydon to Tooting in the early 1920s. (John B.Gent Coll.)

68. The LCC reopened the Cricket Green route in 1926, running cars on an extended service 8 through from Central London via Tooting Junction. At the same time the SMET curtailed their Tooting service from Croydon at Mitcham Fair Green. In this late 1920s view a standard LCC E1 type car waits at the Cricket Green terminus. (Lens of Sutton)

69. Trams ceased in Mitcham in September 1937 when trolleybus routes 612 (Mitcham Fair Green/Battersea) and 630 (West Croydon/Harlesden) were introduced. Shortly before this, former LCC E class car 483 and trolleybus 200 share the road at Fair Green. The trolleybus was on training duties and was also testing the alignment of the new overhead which required the extra traction standards seen here. (J.Bonell)

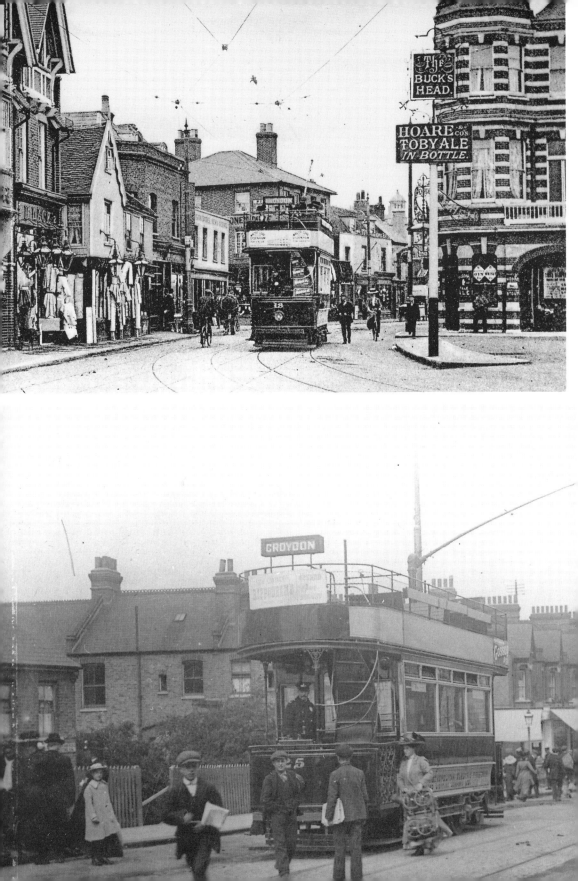

**P.M. times are in heavy figures** | **Croydon - Mitcham - Tooting - Putney - Harrow Road** | **TRAM 30**

Via Tamworth Road, Mitcham Road, Mitcham Common, Tooting, Garratt Lane, Wandsworth, Putney, Fulham Palace Road, Hammersmith, Shepherds Bush, Wood Lane, Wormwood Scrubs

Service interval 5–6 minutes

| | MONDAY to FRIDAY First | MONDAY to FRIDAY Last | SATURDAY First | SATURDAY Last | SUNDAY First | SUNDAY Last |
|---|---|---|---|---|---|---|
| WEST CROYDON *Station* | 4 44 | 11 10  11 32 | 4 44 | 11 30 | 8 7 | 11 8  12 0 |
| Mitcham *Fair Green* | 5 3 | 11 29  11 51 | 5 3 | 11 50 | 8 26 | 11 27  12 19 |
| Tooting *Junction* | 5 9 | 11 35  11 57 | 5 9 | 11 56 | 8 31 | 11 33  12 25 |
| Wandsworth *York Road* | 5 28 | 11 54  12 16 | 5 28 | 12 15 | 8 49 | 11 51  12 43 |
| Putney Bridge | 5 35 | 12 1  12 23 | 5 35 | 12 23 | 8 56 | 11 57  12 49 |
| Hammersmith *Broadway* | 5 47 | 12 13  12 35 | 5 47 | 12 36 | 9 7 | 12 9  1 1 |
| HARROW ROAD *Scrubs Lane* | 6 4 | 12 30 | 6 4 | 12 52 | 9 23 | 12 25 |

| | MONDAY to FRIDAY First | MONDAY to FRIDAY Last | SATURDAY First | SATURDAY Last | SUNDAY First | SUNDAY Last |
|---|---|---|---|---|---|---|
| HARROW ROAD *Scrubs Lane* | 5 24 | 10 48 | 5 25 | 10 51 | 7 39 | 11 8 |
| Hammersmith *Broadway* | 5 0  5 40 | 11 5 | 5 0  5 42 | 11 7 | 7 5  7 55 | 11 24 |
| Putney Bridge | 5 12  5 52 | 11 17 | 5 12  5 54 | 11 20 | 7 16  8 6 | 11 35 |
| Wandsworth *York Road* | 5 19  5 59 | 11 24  11 35 | 5 19  6 1 | 11 28  11 45 | 7 23  8 13 | 11 42 |
| Tooting *Junction* | 5 38  6 18 | 11 43  11 51 | 5 38  6 20 | 11 47  12 4 | 7 41  8 31 | 12 0 |
| Mitcham *Fair Green* | 5 44  6 24 | 11 48  12 0 | 5 44  6 26 | 11 53  12 10 | 7 46  8 35 | 12 6 |
| WEST CROYDON *Station* | 6 3  6 43 | 12 7  12 19 | 6 3  6 45 | 12 12  12 29 | 8 5  8 55 | 12 25 |

70. An early view of SMET car 18 in Mitcham High Street approaching Fair Green from Tooting. The company reported that on three days in 1917 they carried 75,000 people to and from Mitcham Fair. (John B. Gent Coll.)

### MITCHAM ROUTE

**FIRST CARS**

| | WEEKDAYS A.M. | SUNDAYS A.M. |
|---|---|---|
| Aurelia Rd. to Croydon - | 5.56 | 9.19 |
| Canterbury Rd. to Fair Gn. | 5.25 | 8.55 |
| Croydon to Fair Green - | 5.17 | 8.47 |
| Fair Green to Croydon - | 5.45 | 9. 8 |
| Aurelia Rd. to Fair Green | 5.27 | 8.57 |

**LAST CARS**

| | P.M. | P.M. |
|---|---|---|
| Croydon to Fair Green - | 11. 6 | 10.50 |
| Fair Green to Croydon - | 11.28 | 11.15 |
| Fair Green to Aurelia Rd. | 11.28 | 11.15 |
| Croydon to Aurelia Rd. - | 11. 6 | 10.50 |

71. The SMET opened its route to Tooting Junction in 1906, and in 1907 the LCC extended their system to meet the SMET "end on." However the two systems, one using overhead wires and the other below street level conduit, were not then connected. This scene from about 1910 shows SMET car 25 and an LCC A class car at their respective termini. The tracks were connected in 1926 and the LCC provided a plough change pit to enable their cars to work through to Mitcham. The conduit system of current collection is fully described in companion Middleton Press volume *Embankment and Waterloo Tramways*. (John.B.Gent Coll.)

72. In the centre of Croydon a Purley bound tramcar is standing in North End and is about to proceed into High Street. In later London Transport days this was the only single track section to remain between Victoria Embankment and Purley. At peak periods it was used by 38 trams per hour in each direction! There is a junction with the Addiscombe route (right), but the connection was only used for depot working; service cars to Addiscombe terminated just round the corner in George Street (see picture 19). The "Addiscombe Car Waiting" sign was pivoted like a signal arm and was operated by a traffic inspector. The Whitgift Hospital on the right dates from 1596 and is still in use as almshouses. (John B.Gent Coll.)

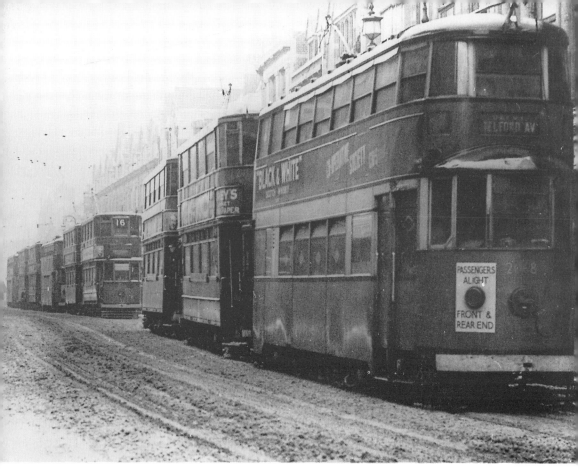

 CROYDON CORPORATION TRAMWAYS

# Cheap Mid-day Fares

The following Cheap Mid-day Fares are now in operation on all Cars leaving Norbury, Thornton Heath, Greyhound, Purley, Selby Road, West Croydon, Addiscombe, and Crown Hill, between the hours of 10 a.m. and 4 p.m., Mondays to Fridays inclusive (Public Holidays excepted).

### BETWEEN

| Norbury | & Greyhound | |
|---|---|---|
| Thornton Hth. | „ Greyhound | |
| Greyhound | „ Purley | **1**d. |
| Selby Road | „ W.Croydon Stn. | |
| Addiscombe | „ Crown Hill | |
| | | |
| Norbury | „ Purley | **2**d. |
| Thornton Hth. | „ Purley | |

5- JAN 1935

T. B. GOODYER.
Tramways Manager.

73. A traffic hold up in snowbound North End during a wartime winter. The leading Feltham tram, car 2068, has a white fender, masked headlamp and netting on the windows with diamond shaped peep holes. This last precaution was to protect passengers from large splinters of glass in the event of a nearby bomb blast. A prominent warning notice signifies that the front exit is still in use, but this facility was discontinued in 1947.
(John B.Gent Coll.)

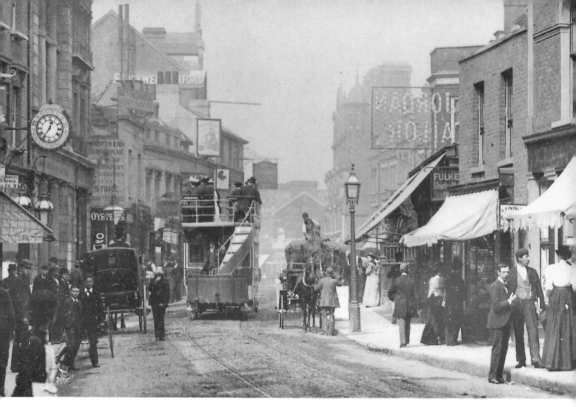

74. The horse car, seen here in North End, was equipped with transverse or "garden" seats. It is on its way to West Croydon in the 1890s. (Photomatic)

75. A pre-1906 view of North End includes single track and loops as car 38, one of the BET's Milnes cars, heads towards Purley. The headlamps on the canopies of these trams were soon moved to the customary position on the dash panels. Note the horse drawn tower wagon. (John B.Gent Coll.)

76. Here we are looking north across the railway bridge at West Croydon in about 1910. Car 21 on the Penge route has come down Oakfield Road, turned into London Road, and will shortly turn into Station Road. When this roundabout working was discontinued in 1926, the north facing curve was retained for depot workings but the curve in the foreground was removed. (Croydon Public Libraries)

PURLEY
BOVRIL
ROYDON
URE HOUSE
MONDAY & THURSDAY
CHILDR
3D
3D
SONS, LIMITED
YMCA
ON.
2

78. Shops and the Southern Railway's 1928 West Croydon Station frontage span the railway bridge in this March 1951 scene. An ex-Croydon E1 type tram on service 42 and a car on service 16 wait at the traffic lights at the Station Road/Tamworth Road crossing. (Pamlin Prints)

77. Now we are looking south along North End from the corner of Station Road as passengers join car 73. Note the smartly turned out official, apparently carrying a point iron. (C.H. Price)

79. London Road, West Croydon in the mid 1930s with Croydon car 367 on the Thornton Heath service. The tram on the right is working from Thornton Heath Depot to take up duty on service 30. As the only connection from Tamworth Road joins the northbound track in London Road, the tram is having to reverse over the crossover to undertake this rather complicated procedure. Two ex-Thomas Tilling buses and another tramcar can also be seen. (Dr. Hugh Nicol)

←——————

80. Plenty of passengers are boarding car 399 at West Croydon in 1947. The driver will probably have to apply sand to negotiate the steep rise away from this stop. The Corporation practice of showing Croydon in larger print than Purley, the ultimate destination, persisted to the end.
(Geoffrey Ashwell)

82. A typical scene was recorded at Broad Green in 1951 with car 394 on service 42 followed by car 2141 on service 18. Services 16 and 18 both worked from Purley to Victoria Embankment with service 16 taking a

81. Croydon bogie car 50 stops at Broad Green. The short bracket arms carrying the overhead are clearly seen but these had to be replaced before LCC through running was introduced as centred overhead was essential for their use of a trailing trolley rope. Barclay & Perkins Foden wagon No.1411 is delivering ample beer supplies to the Star public house.
(C.H.Price)

clockwise course from Kennington and 18 an anti-clockwise one. In 1951 the replacing buses carried route number 109 in both directions.
(John H. Meredith)

83. Car 18 is at Thornton Heath Pond in about 1910. The Thornton Heath route diverged over a single line junction to the right until track rearrangement and doubling in the first part of Brigstock Road in 1924. (Card House)

84. Two LCC E1 class cars were photographed at Thornton Heath Pond in the early days of through running. Twenty of these cars were loaned to Croydon until their own E1 cars were delivered in 1927/8 and were operated by Croydon crews working from Telford Avenue Depot at Streatham. LCC stop signs had by this time replaced the Corporation shields but the list of places served remained for some years. (C.H.Price)

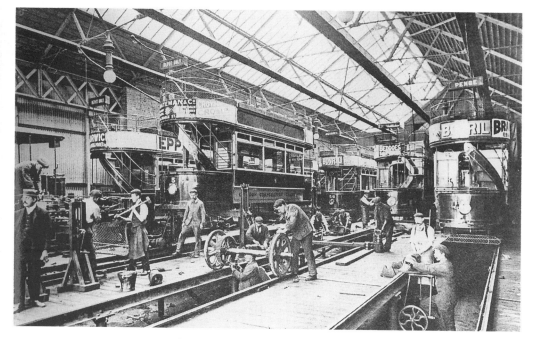

85. Thornton Heath Depot was originally built for horse cars and was extended on electrification. The new section included this workshop and there is much activity in progress. On the extreme left there is a glimpse of Croydon's works car. (John B. Gent Coll.)

86. The same shed in 1938 but no longer a workshop following London Transport's concentration of overhauls for the South London fleet at Charlton. On the right are two ex-Croydon E1 cars, 378 and 393, whilst on the left are two ex-LCC E1 cars, 1493 and 1040, with service 42 stencils. Note that car 1493 has been fitted with screens but the other trams are still to be equipped. (W.A.Camwell)

87. Still at Thornton Heath Pond, Feltham 2136 is proceeding south to Purley while rehabilitated car 398 waits to turn right into Brigstock Road. (D.W.K.Jones)

88. Car 64 is in London Road, Thornton Heath in 1923. The track was then being relaid for through running by LCC cars. Single line working was put into operation on each track in turn and temporary passing loops were laid on ballast beds. The car is going north on the southbound track and the intending passenger appears unsure as to the correct procedure for boarding. Note the"P" for Purley headlamp mask, first introduced as a wartime measure in 1916. (O.J.Morris)

89. Ex-Leyton E3 class car 177 hums along London Road, Norbury, on 1st October 1950. This was the first day that Telford Avenue Depot had a large allocation of this type; they replaced Felthams destined for Leeds, so perhaps the crew had an excuse for getting the "18" stencil back to front. (John H. Meredith)

90. Car 2082 on route 18 passes the track repair gang at Pollards Hill in London Road, Norbury. Compressors and other electrical equipment were fed directly from the overhead line using a long mast and pivoted arm with a contact sitting on top of the overhead wire. (John H. Meredith)

91. Rehabilitated car 1352 is working on service 18x in London Road in 1951. This is a peak hour extra operated from Norwood Depot; this provided one of the few occasions that this type of car worked into the Croydon area. (John H. Meredith)

92. Another Norwood Depot working with car 1991 which was more usually to be seen on Kingsway Subway service 33. Norbury Station bridge in the background had limited headroom and the roadway was first lowered for the opening of the route in 1901 and then again in the 1920s to accommodate top covered cars. (John H. Meredith)

93. Bogie car 55 waits at Norbury Station in 1917. The driver in casual dress is believed to be a member of the office staff helping to alleviate the wartime staff shortage. When the route first opened in 1901, Norbury was almost entirely rural but the shopping parades and housing soon followed the trams.
(O.J. Morris)

94. LCC "Bluebird" car 1 is reversing at Norbury in 1948. Built in 1932 this was a prototype for new rolling stock but plans were thwarted by the formation of the LPTB in 1933. After being used on the Kingsway Subway services, car 1 was transferred to Telford Avenue Depot in 1938 and henceforth worked into Croydon from time to time, usually on peak hour extras. It was sold to Leeds and is now at the National Tramway Museum. This car is fully described in companion volume, *Camberwell & West Norwood Tramways*.
(John B.Gent Coll.)

95. Cars 22 and 64 were recorded at Norbury terminus at Whitsun 1917. An LCC car can be seen behind the two Corporation cars and from 1909 when the LCC route was opened, passengers could change cars to complete a through journey to London. Note that both tracks are in use as a terminal; these were served by a scissors crossover as at Purley. In 1925 the tracks were connected and early in the following year through running between London and Purley commenced.
(O.J. Morris)

# 8 Thornton Heath Pond to Thornton Heath

96. Bogie car 51 is turning into Brigstock Road in about 1905. On the opposite side of the road the unnumbered 1902 works car is standing on the entrance track to Thornton Heath Depot whilst just beyond is Brigstock Villa , the headquarters of the Croydon Corporation Tramways Department. Also evident are feeder cables and an indication of the discomfort offered by alternative forms of road transport. (John B.Gent Coll.)

97. Car 368 is leaving the first loop in Brigstock Road bound for Croydon. This is a rebuild of one of the Croydon open top bogie cars and, with its nine sister vehicles, formed the mainstay of the Thornton Heath service between 1928 and 1936. (G.N. Southerden)

98. Further along Brigstock Road interlaced track was provided instead of single track. Car 395 is sharing road space with a parade of cubs and scouts on a Sunday morning in March 1949. Note the TRAM PINCH warning for motorists. (John H.Meredith)

# CROYDON POST AND TELEGRAPH OFFICE.

Money Order Office, Inland Revenue Stamp Office, Post Office, Savings Bank, and Insurance and Annuity Office.

HEAD OFFICE—HIGH STREET.  Postmaster—E. L. WESTELL.

Week-days—8 a.m.—8 p.m.
Sundays, Christmas Day and Good Friday.—9—10.30 a.m., 5—6 p.m.
Bank Holidays.—9—12 noon and 5—7 p.m.

### TRAMCAR LETTER BOX CONNECTIONS.

For the convenience of residents in the Croydon Postal Area who may have urgent correspondence to post after the final general clearance from street letter boxes has been effected, posting receptacles are provided on tramcars leaving :—

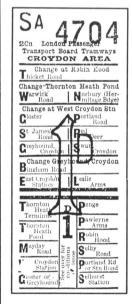

| MONDAYS TO FRIDAYS. | | | |
|---|---|---|---|
| — | | Car Returning from Outer Termini. | Due at West Croydon Station on Return. |
| WEST CROYDON STATION for: | p.m. | p.m. | p.m. |
| PURLEY - - - - - | 10.15 | 10.36 | 10.56 |
| THORNTON HEATH - - - | 10.23 | 10.38 | 10.53 |
| PENGE - - - - - | 10. 5 | 10.34 | 11. 0 |

| SUNDAYS. | | | |
|---|---|---|---|
| — | | Car Returning from Outer Termini. | Due at West Croydon Station on Return. |
| WEST CROYDON STATION for: | p.m. | p.m. | p.m. |
| PURLEY - - - - | 7.20 | 7.34 | 7.50 |
|  | 9.10 | 9.30 | 9.46 |
| THORNTON HEATH - - | 7.30 | 7.45 | 8. 0 |
|  | 9.20 | 9.35 | 9.50 |
| PENGE - - - - | 7.11 | 7.37 | 8. 3 |
|  | 8.53 | 9.21 | 9.47 |

Both on the outward and the inward journey, persons having letters to post may hail the Motorman to stop the car at the stopping places.

The tramcars that are used for the above purpose will be distinguished by an illuminated **SIGN** bearing the words "**POST CAR.**" This sign will be fixed against the window above the step to the front platform. The **Letter Box** will be found at the front of the car on the outward and the back on the inward journeys. The sign, "Post Car," is not shown on the cars to and from Purley.

99. Another Sunday, 9th May 1948, and the same interlaced track carries former LCC HR2 class car 1885. The car is on hire to the Southern Counties Touring Society for an enthusiasts tour and it is probably the only occasion when this type of tram ventured into Croydon. (John B.Gent Coll.)

100. Car 391 breasts the railway bridge at Thornton Heath station; this vehicle had received flush panelling on both decks during a major overhaul in 1948, the only ex-Croydon car to be so treated. This station is featured in the *Victoria to East Croydon* album from Middleton Press. (D.A.Thompson)

101. Cars 392 and 1906 belong to the ex-Croydon E1 and ex-LCC E3 classes respectively. They are seen here in Thornton Heath High Street in 1949. At that time Thornton Heath depot's allocation consisted of these two types of car and they were used indiscriminately on services 16, 18 and 42. (H.B.Priestley)

102. Car 33 is in Thornton Heath High Street in this pre-First World War photograph. The tram will reverse at the end of the High Street, but its destination blind has already been changed. On the right is an early cinema, the patrons of which brought extra tramway revenue. (John B.Gent Coll.)

103. A Corporation E1 class car stands at Thornton Heath terminus around 1930. The car's route number stencils and side boards proclaim ROUTE 2. THORNTON HEATH HIGH STREET AND CROYDON (GREYHOUND). The use of this type of tram on route 2 was normally confined to Saturdays at that time. Croydon's route 2 became 42 under the LPTB regime in 1934 to avoid duplication with the Victoria Embankment/ Wimbledon service. (G.N.Southerden)

104. Until 1936 Thornton Heath cars terminated at the intersection of High Street, Whitehorse Road and Whitehorse Lane. The tramway was extended a short distance along the old Whitehorse Road route and a new crossover was installed. This was one of the rare LT examples of positive thinking to ease traffic congestion allegedly caused by the tramways. In this 1949 view, car 390 has negotiated the crossover and is about to make its return journey to Croydon. Service 42 was latterly one of the three most frequent on the London system, with 20 trams per hour at peak periods and sometimes extras on Saturday afternoons for football traffic at Selhurst Park. (H.B.Priestley)

## CROYDON CORPORATION TRAMWAYS.

## NOTICE.

### Extension of Thornton Heath Route

On and after **WEDNESDAY NEXT**, the 7th instant, and until further notice, the Purley and Thornton Heath Service will be extended, and Cars will run to and from the "GLO'STER," WHITEHORSE ROAD, as follows:

#### Week-Days.

| FROM | TO | WORK-PEOPLE'S CARS | | SERVICE CARS | |
|---|---|---|---|---|---|
| | | First Car | Service | First Car | Last Car |
| "Glo'ster" | Purley | 4.58 a.m | 20 mins | 7 18 a.m 7 25 a.m | 10 50 p.m |
| "Glo'ster" | "Red Deer" only | | | 7.50 a.m 10 mins | 10 40 a.m |
| Purley | "Glo'ster" | 5.10 a.m | 20 mins | 7.10 a.m 7.25 a.m | 10 50 p.m |
| "Red Deer" | "Glo'ster" | | | 7.40 a.m 10 mins | 11.20 a.m |

\*Also at 10.55, 11 0, and 11.10 p.m to Purley Depot only.
†Also at 11.5 and 11.25 p.m., to Pond only.

#### Sundays.

| FROM | TO | First Car | Service | Last Car |
|---|---|---|---|---|
| "Glo'ster" | Purley | 8 55 a.m | 10 mins and 11 a.m and then 5 mins apart | 10 35 p.m |
| "Glo'ster" | "Red Deer" only | 8 50 a.m | 10 mins | 11 0 a.m |
| Purley | "Glo'ster" | 9 5 a.m | 10 mins and 11 a.m then 5 mins | 10 35 p.m |
| "Red Deer" | "Glo'ster" | 9 0 a.m | 10 mins | 11 40 a.m |

†Also at 10 45 p.m., to Pond only.

NOTE. Cars take 5 minutes to run between "Glo'ster" and Thornton Heath (Whitehorse Lane)
Work-People's Tickets will be issued on all Cars up to
7.25 a.m. from "Glo'ster," and 7.35 a.m from Purley.

For Fares, and Times of Afternoon Work-People's Cars, see other side

Tramway Offices.  T B GOODYER.
Thornton Heath.  Tramways Manager.
*November, 1906.*

---

| CROYDON - THORNTON HEATH | | | | | TRAM 42 |
|---|---|---|---|---|---|

Service interval : WEEKDAYS 3-4 mins. (evening 5 mins.), SUNDAY morning 7 minutes (before 9 a.m. 15 mins.), afternoon and evening 5 mins.

| | WEEKDAYS | | SUNDAY | | | | | | | | |
|---|---|---|---|---|---|---|---|---|---|---|---|
| | First | Last | First | Last | | | | | | | |
| CROYDON *High Street, Coombe Road* | .... 5 51 | 11 33 | .... 7 20 | 11 33 | .... | .... | .... | .... | ... | .... | |
| WEST CROYDON *Station* | 5 59 | 11 41 | .. 7 28 | 11 41 | .. | .. | .. | .. | .. | .... | |
| THORNTON HEATH *Pond* | 5 21 6 4 | 11 46 | 6 51 7 33 | 11 46 | .. | .... | .... | .... | .... | .... | |
| THORNTON HEATH *Whitehorse Road* | 5 28 6 11 | 11 53 | 6 58 7 40 | 11 53 | .. | .. | .. | .. | .. | .... | |
| THORNTON HEATH *Whitehorse Road* | 5 31 .... | 11 13 11 55 | 7 0 .... | 11 13 11 55 | .... | | | | | | |
| THORNTON HEATH *Pond* | 5 38 .... | 11 20 12 2 | 7 7 .... | 11 20 12 2 | .. | .. | .. | .. | .. | .. | |
| WEST CROYDON *Station* | 5 43 .... | 11 25 .... | 7 12 .... | 11 25 | .... | .. | .. | .. | .. | .... | |
| CROYDON *High Street, Coombe Road* | .. 5 51 .. | 11 33 .. | 7 20 .. | 11 33 | .. | .. | .. | .. | .. | .... | |

# 9 Whitehorse Road

105. The tramway along the section of Whitehorse Road between the Gloster and Thornton Heath had a very chequered career. Its horse tramway opened in 1881 and lasted just eight years, whilst its electric service operated for only two brief spells from 1906 to 1908, and from 1910 to 1913. This view of Whitehorse Road was taken from the tower of St.Alban's Church which stands at the end of Thornton Heath High Street, but is officially in South Norwood! The crossover installed in 1936 (see picture 104) was located where the three people are standing in the roadway.
(John B.Gent Coll.)

106. During the 1906/8 period the Thornton Heath service was worked as a circular route, out via Brigstock Road, returning via Whitehorse Road, and vice-versa. Car 22 is in Whitehorse Road at the Broadway and is returning to West Croydon on this circular service.   (John B.Gent Coll.)

107. Also in Whitehorse Road, this view is at the Gloster and shows car 23 approaching the junction with the Penge and Crystal Palace routes which are seen diverging to the right. The tram is carrying a VIA GLOSTER board under the canopy. Ironically this was the only lengthy double tracked section of the Corporation's system away from the main road route. (Card House)

# 10 Rolling Stock

## CROYDON CORPORATION

| | |
|---|---|
| –35 | 4 wheel double deck canopied open top cars with reversed stairs by G.F. Milnes 1901<br>16 were mounted on Peckham cantilever trucks (1–8,11,12,15,23–26,35)<br>19 were mounted on Brill 21E trucks (Some exchanges of trucks occurred later)<br>3 rebuilt with normal stairs (25,34,35)<br>All withdrawn 1927 with 4 sold to SMET (13,25,34,35) |
| 6–55 | 8 wheel double deck short canopied open top cars with double flight stairs by G.F. Milnes 1902<br>Mounted on Brill 22E maximum traction trucks<br>Fitted with air brakes and top covers c.1928 and renumbered 21–30, classified B/2<br>'E' added to fleet numbers by London Transport 1933 and then renumbered 365–374 as each car went to Charlton<br>for overhaul<br>Withdrawn 1936/37 |
| 6–45*<br>6–75* | 4 wheel double deck canopied open top cars with normal stairs by Brush 1906–11<br>Mounted on Brill 21E trucks or of similar design by Brush or Mountain & Gibson<br>10 withdrawn 1927 (43,44,62,63,64,66,67,69 for sale to SMET and 41,57 for breaking up)<br>Remainder renumbered 1–20 in reverse order of their previous numbers, classified W/1<br>'E' added to fleet numbers by London Transport 1933 and 1,2,3,5,11 later renumbered 345,346,347,349,355<br>Withdrawn 1933–36 |
| 1–55 | 8 wheel double deck top covered cars by Hurst Nelson 1927/28, classified E/1<br>Mounted on Hurst Nelson maximum traction trucks<br>'E' added to fleet numbers by London Transport 1933 and later renumbered 375–399<br>376,379,380,398 'rehabilitated' 1936<br>All fitted with windscreens by 1939<br>396 withdrawn after bomb damage 1941, 376 withdrawn after fire damage 1945, remainder transferred to New Cross<br>Depot 1951 and withdrawn 1951/52 |
| orks<br>car | Unnumbered 4 wheel water car by United Electric Car Co. 1907<br>Mounted on Brill 21E truck<br>Rebuilt as welding car and water tank removed 1916<br>Numbered 056 by London Transport and transferred to West Ham Depot<br>Withdrawn 1937 |

For details of earlier cars numbered 36–45 and 56–60 see SMET table

108. The ten bogie cars 46 - 55 were built in 1902 and they formed the backbone of the main line service between Norbury and Purley. They also worked via Brigstock Road to Thornton Heath, but they did not stray on to the Penge or Addiscombe lines. Note the roller bearing axle boxes and the lower saloon curtains in this early view of car 52.
(John B.Gent Coll.)

109. Croydon Corporation had visions of equipping their original bogie cars to work through to Central London, but this was not to be. Instead they rebuilt them with ungainly top covers in 1928 and put them to work on the Thornton Heath service, where they continued until replaced by ex-LCC E1 cars in 1936/7. Note that two trolley poles have now been fitted to avoid swinging a single pole at the termini. (A.J.Watkins Coll.)

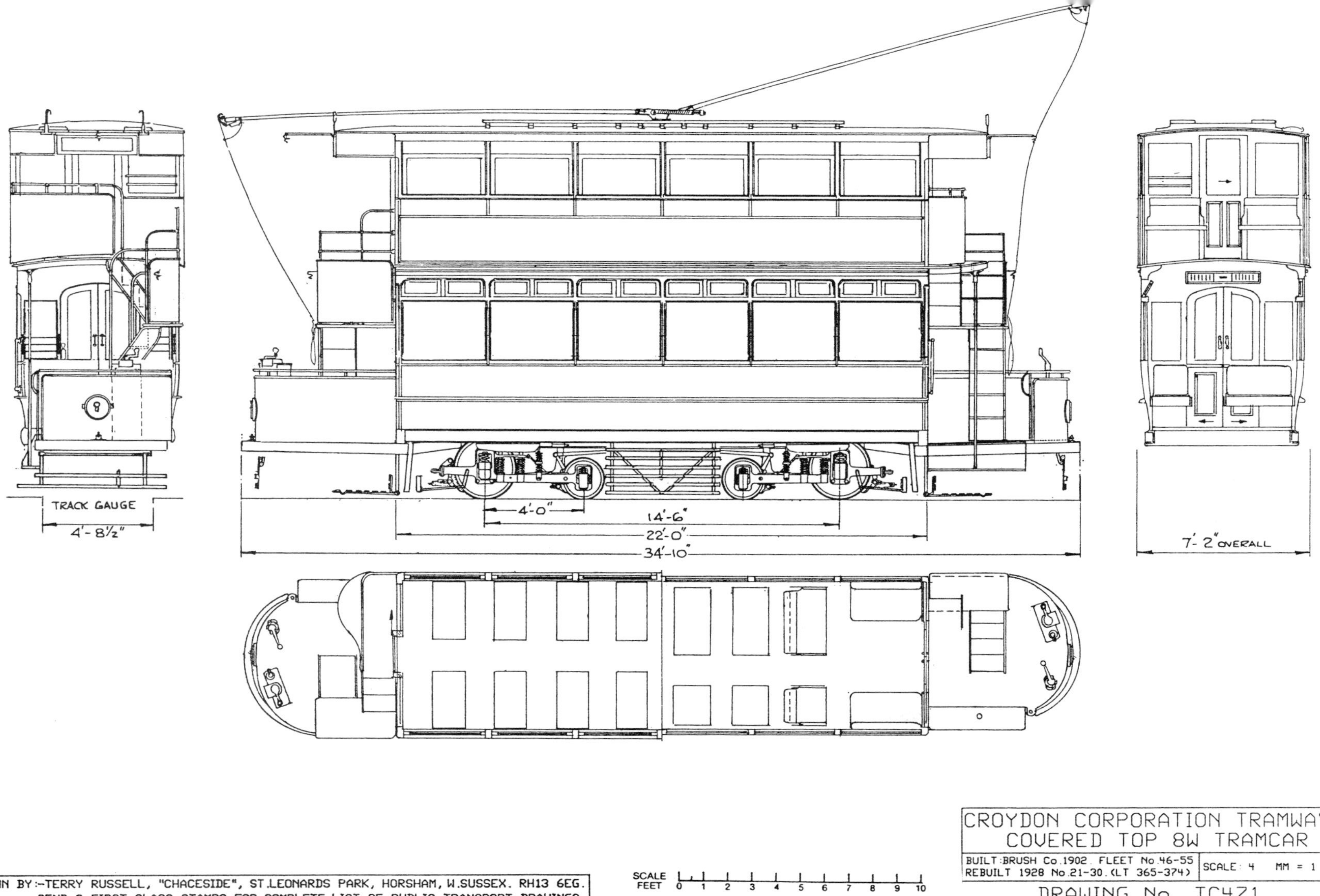

CROYDON CORPORATION TRAMWAYS
COVERED TOP 8W TRAMCAR

BUILT BRUSH Co 1902 FLEET No 46-55 SCALE: 4 MM = 1 FOOT
REBUILT 1928 No 21-30 (LT 365-374)

DRAWING No. TC471

SCALE
FEET 0 1 2 3 4 5 6 7 8 9 10

7'-2" overall

14'-6"
22'-0"
34'-10"
4'-0"

TRACK GAUGE
4'-8½"

DRAWN BY:- TERRY RUSSELL, "CHACESIDE", ST LEONARDS PARK, HORSHAM, W.SUSSEX. RH13 6EG.
SEND 3 FIRST CLASS STAMPS FOR COMPLETE LIST OF PUBLIC TRANSPORT DRAWINGS.

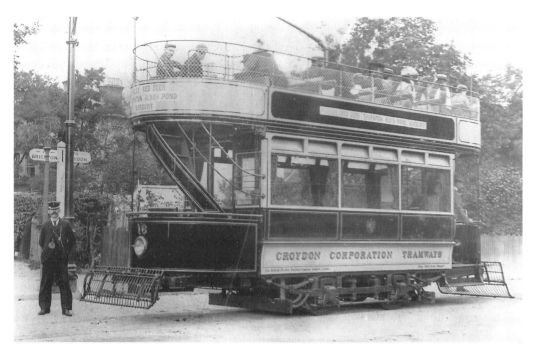

110. One of the 35 four wheel trams of 1901, car 16 is seen in original condition with Providence lifeguards and paper stickers giving route details. The lifeguards were condemned by the Board of Trade inspecting officer and they were soon replaced by more conventional fittings. This car is mounted on a Brill 21E truck. (John B.Gent Coll.)

111. The later series of 30 four wheel cars were built in three batches between 1906 and 1911. This was car 42 of the first batch and this particular vehicle was renumbered 15 in 1927. (C.F.Klapper)

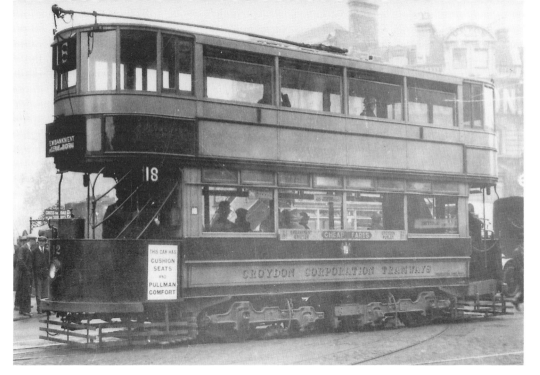

112. Croydon Corporation car 42 was photographed when new in 1928. These cars were an updated version of the LCC 1907 design. The poster at the back of the platform proclaims THIS CAR HAS CUSHION SEATS AND PULLMAN COMFORT. Note the plough carrier attached to one of the trucks, as was then standard LCC practice. The unrestrained movement of the trucks tended to damage the ploughs so body mounted carriers were soon substituted, with most of the 25 cars so equipped when the LPTB took over in 1933. (G.N.Southerden)

113. The cushion seats are seen in the lower saloon of car 394. The main windows were fixed and the quarter lights on each side were opened in unison by turning the handle on the centre pillar. The bulkhead door (slid open in this view) and the side panel were glazed with yellow tinted glass to reduce the glare from the lower saloon lights on the driver's windscreen. (V.C.Jones)

## SOUTH METROPOLITAN ELECTRIC TRAMWAYS

| | | |
|---|---|---|
| 1–16 | 4 wheel double deck canopied open top cars with normal stairs by United Electric Car Co. 1906<br>Mounted on Brush long wheelbase radial trucks | Later classified **Type J** |
| | Withdrawn 1935 | |
| 17–26 | 4 wheel double deck canopied open top cars with normal stairs by G.F. Milnes 1902<br>Mounted on Milnes trucks | Later classified **Type K** |
| | Originally numbered **36–45** in the Croydon District fleet<br>Withdrawn 1927–34 | |
| 27–29, 31,35 | 8 wheel double deck short canopied open top cars with double flight stairs by Brush 1902<br>Mounted on reversed Brush maximum traction trucks | Later classified **Type L** |
| | Originally numbered **56–60** in the Croydon District fleet<br>Withdrawn 1931 but stored at Fulwell then broken up 1934 | |
| 30, 32–34 | 8 wheel double deck canopied open top cars with reversed stairs by Dick Kerr 1902<br>Mounted on reversed Brill 22E maximum traction trucks | Later classified **Type O** |
| | Purchased in 1906/07 from Gravesend and Northfleet Tramways<br>Withdrawn 1931 but stored at Fulwell then broken up 1934 | |
| 36–51 | 4 wheel double deck canopied open top cars with normal stairs built by Brush 1906<br>Mounted on Brush short wheelbase trucks | Later classified **Type M** |
| | **47** loaned to MET 1927 and became their rail grinder **04** with top deck removed<br>Remainder withdrawn 1936 | |
| 17,21, 47,52 | The SMET bought 12 cars from Croydon Corporation in 1927 (13,25,34,35,43,44,62,63,64,66,67,69)<br>Only 4 entered service on the SMET: 17(64), 21(66), 47(44), 52(67) | Classified **Type P** |
| | **17** was at first numbered **53**<br>**13** sold to LUT and became their rail grinder **006** with top deck removed but stairs retained<br>**43,69** loaned to MET and became their breakdown car **07** and salt car **09** both with top decks removed<br>**25,34,35,62,63** were used for spares<br>The 4 SMET operational cars withdrawn 1934 | |
| Works car | Unnumbered 4 wheel water car built by Brush 1902<br>Mounted on Brush truck<br>Sold, presumably for use elsewhere, prior to 1912 | |

SMET cars taken over by London Transport in 1933 received an **'S'** suffix to their fleet numbers but none was renumbere
in the London Transport series

114. SMET cars 1 to 16 were built in 1906 and were four wheel cars on long wheelbase trucks. Some wre originally fitted with track brakes for the Crystal Palace route, but they caused excessive wear on the curves at the Robin Hood junction. The whole class was then placed on the Sutton route and they remained there for the rest of their lives.
(John B.Gent Coll.)

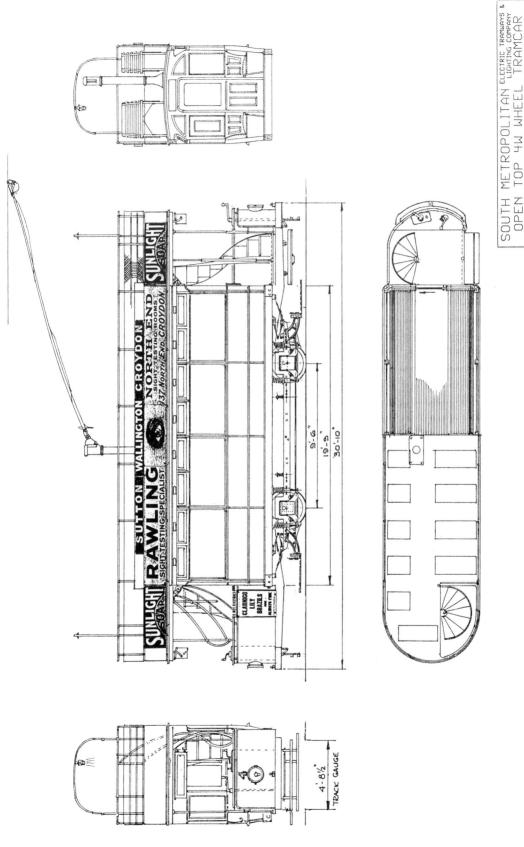

SOUTH METROPOLITAN ELECTRIC TRAMWAYS & LIGHTING COMPANY

OPEN TOP 4W WHEEL TRAMCAR

TYPE "J". BUILT : BRUSH 1906

FLEET NO. 1 — 16.

SCALE 4    MM = 1 FOOT

DRAWING No. TC473

SUNLIGHT SOAP

RAWLING
SIGHT TESTING SPECIALIST

NORTH END
SIGHT TESTING ROOMS
33, NORTH END, CROYDON

SUTTON  WALLINGTON  CROYDON

SUNLIGHT SOAP

CLARNICO
LILY
BRAZILS
ALWAYS FINE

9'-6"
19'-9"
30'-10"

4'-8½"
TRACK GAUGE

SCALE
FEET   0  1  2  3  4  5  6  7  8  9  10  11  12

DRAWN BY:- TERRY RUSSELL, "CHACESIDE", ST LEONARDS PARK, HORSHAM, W.SUSSEX. RH13 6EG.
SEND 3 FIRST CLASS STAMPS FOR COMPLETE LIST OF PUBLIC TRANSPORT DRAWINGS.

115. Believed to be car 21, this is one of the ten four wheel cars owned by the BET and built in 1902 for the Croydon services. Soon after the SMET took over in 1906, another of the batch, car 19, overturned at Carshalton causing two fatalities (the only serious accident on the SMET). As a consequence these cars were then confined to the flatter Mitcham route. The hoops at the ends of the top decks of SMET cars were fitted from 1916 onwards to protect passengers from trolley poles being turned in the wartime blackout. (W.Gratwicke)

116. Car 28 was one of the five bogie trams constructed in 1902; they were owned by the BET. The bodies were similar to Croydon Corporation bogie cars, but they had different trucks which did not perform satisfactorily. They were used only on the Mitcham route. (W.Gratwicke)

Some 153 different trams are listed in the two rolling stock tables. However, around 500 other tramcars of various classes and types have operated in or have visited the Croydon area, the list includes:

| | |
|---|---|
| Leyton: E3 | MET: E, UCC car 2167 |
| LCC: E, E1, EI 500 series, | Walthamstow: cars 2042 - 2061 |
| HR2, car 1 | West Ham: cars 66, 327 - 330 |
| LUT: U, UCC (Feltham) | London Transport: E1 rehab. |
| | Sundry works cars |

117. The SMET purchased four large eight wheel cars from another BET tramway, the Gravesend & Northfleet company, in 1906/7. Originally they were fitted with reversed stairs, but car 34 is seen here after it had been rebuilt with normal direct stairs, with higher sheeting to the upper deck. It also displays the fleet name SOUTHMET which latterly appeared on all the system's cars. These trams were also confined to the Mitcham route.
(W.Gratwicke)

118. Cars 36 to 51 were a shortened version of cars 1 to 16. After initial use on the Sutton route, they were transferred to the Crystal Palace route and they were equipped with Spencer track brakes for use in descending Anerley Hill. The company' full name appears on the waist panel in this 1918 photograph.
(W.Gratwicke)

119. Car 52 is smartly turned out; until 1927 it was Croydon Corporation car 67. It was purchased with three others to be used for short workings on the Mitcham and Sutton services. (Topical Press)

# 11 Finale

120. Saturday 7th April 1951 was a sad day for local tramway enthusiasts. The last car ran late in the evening with large crowds in the streets to bid it farewell. During the day, the Light Railway Transport League hired car 1 for a tour which included a run to Highgate and trips out to Purley and Thornton Heath. The tram is seen here on the interlaced track in Brigstock Road on its way to Thornton Heath. Car 379 waits to enter the section a few hours before service 42 was replaced by RT buses on route 190. (John H.Meredith)

# 12 Croydon Tramlink

The Croydon Tramlink Act was passed in 1994, over 43 years after the last tram had run in the town. Work started in January 1997 on relocating and diverting underground equipment. The railway lines between Wimbledon and West Croydon and between Addiscombe and Elmers End closed in May 1997 for incorporation in the tramway. Construction started in August 1997; completion and opening of the system was planned for November 1999.

Croydon Tramlink replaces trains between Wimbledon and West Croydon, with new single track flyovers crossing the Railtrack lines at Mitcham Junction and Wandle Park, Croydon. Trams then run through the streets on a single track clockwise loop from Cairo New Road (Pitlake) via Tamworth Road (see illustrations 47, 48, 49 and 50), Station Road (see illustration 28) and Wellesley Road to George Street, eastbound, and from George Street via Crown Hill, and Church Street (westbound).

In George Street (east) trams run on double track reservation along the former eastbound carriageway to a three track tram station outside East Croydon station (see illustration 21). There is double track street running along Addiscombe Road for about half a mile, then a short section of roadside running to Sandilands before the tracks descend to a junction and enter the cutting of the former Woodside and South Croydon Railway which closed in 1983.

Southbound the route follows the former railway alignment for about half a mile through three short tunnels and then turns sharply into Lloyd Park. From here the totally new alignment is a mixture of roadside and cross-country reservation through woodland and open country with steep gradients to New Addington, a large community with a population of some 23,000 and situated on the North Downs, some 130 metres above central Croydon.

Northbound from Sandilands the route follows the former railway alignment to Arena, a point midway between Woodside and Elmers End. One single track line continues the short distance to Elmers End, whilst a new link across South Norwood Country Park allows trams to join the alignment of the Crystal Palace to Beckenham Junction railway near Birkbeck. Trams then run, mainly on single track, alongside trains to Beckenham Junction and terminate just outside the station.

The routes are:
1 Wimbledon - Croydon - Elmers End
2 Croydon - Beckenham Junction
3 Croydon - New Addington

There are 38 stations on the 28km system and the 24 trams are housed in a new depot at Therapia Lane, a short distance from the old Southmet depot at Aurelia Road. In 1999 trams return to Croydon over some interesting and scenically attractive routes with several sections of single and interlaced track.

121.   Heads turn to watch 2530 descending Crown Hill in the centre of Croydon. The car is on a routine test run on 13th August 1999. Based on trams already in operation in Cologne, the vehicles have seats for 70 and can accommodate 130 standing passengers. The fleet numbers 2530 to 2553 run on consecutively from the highest numbered London Transport tram. (John H.Meredith)

## Middleton Press

Easebourne Lane, Midhurst, W Sussex. GU29 9AZ Tel: 01730 813169 Fax: 01730 812601
Email: enquiries@middletonpress.fsnet.co.uk *If books are not available from your local transport stockist, order direct with cheque, Visa or Mastercard, post free UK.*

### BRANCH LINES
Branch Line to Allhallows
Branch Line to Alton
Branch Lines around Ascot
Branch Line to Ashburton
Branch Lines around Bodmin
Branch Line to Bude
Branch Lines around Canterbury
Branch Lines around Chard & Yeovil
Branch Line to Cheddar
Branch Lines around Cromer
Branch Line to the Derwent Valley
Branch Lines to East Grinstead
Branch Lines of East London
Branch Lines to Effingham Junction
Branch Lines around Exmouth
Branch Lines to Falmouth, Helston & St. Ives
Branch Line to Fairford
Branch Lines around Gosport
Branch Line to Hayling
Branch Lines to Henley, Windsor & Marlow
Branch Line to Hawkhurst
Branch Line to Ilfracombe
Branch Line to Kingsbridge
Branch Line to Kingswear
Branch Line to Lambourn
Branch Lines to Launceston & Princetown
Branch Lines to Longmoor
Branch Line to Looe
Branch Line to Lyme Regis
Branch Line to Lynton
Branch Lines around March
Branch Lines around Midhurst
Branch Line to Minehead
Branch Line to Moretonhampstead
Branch Lines to Newport (IOW)
Branch Lines to Newquay
Branch Lines around North Woolwich
Branch Line to Padstow
Branch Lines around Plymouth
Branch Lines to Princes Risborough
Branch Lines to Seaton and Sidmouth
Branch Lines around Sheerness
Branch Line to Shrewsbury
Branch Line to Swanage *updated*
Branch Line to Tenterden
Branch Lines around Tiverton
Branch Lines to Torrington
Branch Lines to Tunbridge Wells
Branch Line to Upwell
Branch Lines of West London
Branch Lines of West Wiltshire
Branch Lines around Weymouth
Branch Lines around Wimborne
Branch Lines around Wisbech

### NARROW GAUGE
Branch Line to Lynton
Branch Lines around Portmadoc 1923-46
Branch Lines around Porthmadog 1954-94
Branch Line to Southwold
Douglas to Port Erin
Douglas to Peel
Kent Narrow Gauge
Northern France Narrow Gauge
Romneyrail
Southern France Narrow Gauge
Sussex Narrow Gauge
Surrey Narrow Gauge
Swiss Narrow Gauge
Two-Foot Gauge Survivors
Vivarais Narrow Gauge

### SOUTH COAST RAILWAYS
Ashford to Dover
Bournemouth to Weymouth
Brighton to Worthing
Eastbourne to Hastings
Hastings to Ashford
Portsmouth to Southampton
Ryde to Ventnor
Southampton to Bournemouth

### SOUTHERN MAIN LINES
Basingstoke to Salisbury
Bromley South to Rochester
Crawley to Littlehampton
Dartford to Sittingbourne
East Croydon to Three Bridges
Epsom to Horsham
Exeter to Barnstaple
Exeter to Tavistock
Faversham to Dover
London Bridge to East Croydon
Orpington to Tonbridge
Tonbridge to Hastings
Salisbury to Yeovil
Sittingbourne to Ramsgate
Swanley to Ashford
Tavistock to Plymouth
Three Bridges to Brighton
Victoria to Bromley South
Victoria to East Croydon
Waterloo to Windsor
Waterloo to Woking
Woking to Portsmouth
Woking to Southampton
Yeovil to Exeter

### EASTERN MAIN LINES
Barking to Southend
Ely to Kings Lynn
Ely to Norwich
Fenchurch Street to Barking
Hitchin to Peterborough
Ilford to Shenfield
Ipswich to Saxmundham
Liverpool Street to Ilford
Saxmundham to Yarmouth
Tilbury Loop

### WESTERN MAIN LINES
Bristol to Taunton
Didcot to Banbury
Didcot to Swindon
Ealing to Slough
Exeter to Newton Abbot
Newton Abbot to Plymouth
Newbury to Westbury
Paddington to Ealing
Paddington to Princes Risborough
Plymouth to St. Austell
Princes Risborough to Banbury
Reading to Didcot
Slough to Newbury
St. Austell to Penzance
Swindon to Bristol
Taunton to Exeter
Westbury to Taunton

### MIDLAND MAIN LINES
St. Albans to Bedford
Euston to Harrow & Wealdstone
St. Pancras to St. Albans

### COUNTRY RAILWAY ROUTES
Abergavenny to Merthyr
Andover to Southampton
Bath to Evercreech Junction
Bath Green Park to Bristol
Burnham to Evercreech Junction
Cheltenham to Andover
Croydon to East Grinstead
Didcot to Winchester
East Kent Light Railway
Fareham to Salisbury
Frome to Bristol
Guildford to Redhill
Reading to Basingstoke
Reading to Guildford
Redhill to Ashford
Salisbury to Westbury
Stratford upon Avon to Cheltenham
Strood to Paddock Wood
Taunton to Barnstaple
Wenford Bridge to Fowey
Westbury to Bath
Woking to Alton
Yeovil to Dorchester

### GREAT RAILWAY ERAS
Ashford from Steam to Eurostar
Clapham Junction 50 years of change
Festiniog in the Fifties
Festiniog in the Sixties
Festiniog 50 years of enterprise
Isle of Wight Lines 50 years of change
Railways to Victory 1944-46
Return to Blaenau 1970-82
SECR Centenary album
Talyllyn 50 years of change
Wareham to Swanage 50 years of change
Yeovil 50 years of change

### LONDON SUBURBAN RAILWAYS
Caterham and Tattenham Corner
Charing Cross to Dartford
Clapham Jn. to Beckenham Jn.
Crystal Palace (HL) & Catford Loop
East London Line
Finsbury Park to Alexandra Palace
Holbourn Viaduct to Lewisham
Kingston and Hounslow Loops
Lewisham to Dartford
Lines around Wimbledon
Liverpool Street to Chingford
London Bridge to Addiscombe
Mitcham Junction Lines
North London Line
South London Line
West Croydon to Epsom
West London Line
Willesden Junction to Richmond
Wimbledon to Beckenham
Wimbledon to Epsom

### STEAMING THROUGH
Steaming through Cornwall
Steaming through the Isle of Wight
Steaming through Kent
Steaming through West Hants

### TRAMWAY CLASSICS
Aldgate & Stepney Tramways
Barnet & Finchley Tramways
Bath Tramways
Brighton's Tramways
Bristol's Tramways
Burton & Ashby Tramways
Camberwell & W.Norwood Tramways
Clapham & Streatham Tramways
Croydon's Tramways
Dover's Tramways
East Ham & West Ham Tramways
Edgware and Willesden Tramways
Eltham & Woolwich Tramways
Embankment & Waterloo Tramways
Exeter & Taunton Tramways
Fulwell - Home to Trams, Trolleys and Buses
Great Yarmouth Tramways
Greenwich & Dartford Tramways
Hammersmith & Hounslow Tramways
Hampstead & Highgate Tramways
Hastings Tramways
Holborn & Finsbury Tramways
Ilford & Barking Tramways
Kingston & Wimbledon Tramways
Lewisham & Catford Tramways
Liverpool Tramways 1. Eastern Routes
Liverpool Tramways 2. Southern Routes
Liverpool Tramways 3. Northern Routes
Maidstone & Chatham Tramways
Margate to Ramsgate
North Kent Tramways
Norwich Tramways
Reading Tramways
Seaton & Eastbourne Tramways
Shepherds Bush & Uxbridge Tramways
Southend-on-sea Tramways
South London Line Tramways 1903-33
Southwark & Deptford Tramways
Stamford Hill Tramways
Twickenham & Kingston Tramways
Victoria & Lambeth Tramways
Waltham Cross & Edmonton Tramways
Walthamstow & Leyton Tramways
Wandsworth & Battersea Tramways

### TROLLEYBUS CLASSICS
Croydon Trolleybuses
Derby Trolleybuses
Hastings Trolleybuses
Huddersfield Trolleybuses
Maidstone Trolleybuses
Portsmouth Trolleybuses
Reading Trolleybuses
Woolwich & Dartford Trolleybuses

### WATERWAY ALBUMS
Kent and East Sussex Waterways
London to Portsmouth Waterway
West Sussex Waterways

### MILITARY BOOKS
Battle over Portsmouth
Battle over Sussex 1940
Blitz over Sussex 1941-42
Bombers over Sussex 1943-45
Bognor at War
Military Defence of West Sussex
Military Signals from the South Coast
Secret Sussex Resistance
Surrey Home Guard

### OTHER RAILWAY BOOKS
Index to all Middleton Press stations
Industrial Railways of the South-East
South Eastern & Chatham Railways
London Chatham & Dover Railway
London Termini - Past and Proposed
War on the Line (SR 1939-45)

### BIOGRAPHY
Garraway Father & Son